ABILENE LAWMEN

The Smith-Hickok Years
1870-71

Larry D. Underwood

Dageforde Publishing, Inc

Western History from Dageforde Publishing, Inc.

ISBN 1-886225-40-0

Cover design by Angie Johnson Art Productions.

Library of Congress Cataloging-in-Publication Data
Underwood, Larry.
     Abilene lawmen : the Smith-Hickok years, 1870-71 / Larry D. Underwood.
     p. cm.
     Includes bibliographical references and index.
     ISBN 1-886225-40-0 (alk. paper)
     1. Smith, Thomas James, 1830-1870. 2. Hickok, Wild Bill, 1837-1876. 3. Peace officers—Kansas—Abilene Biography. 4. Frontier and pioneer life—Kansas—Abilene. 5. Law enforcement—Kansas—Abilene—History—19th century. 6. Abilene (Kan.)—History—19th century.
     F689.A2 U64 1999
     363.2'09781'56—dc21   99-35308
                                                                        CIP

DAGEFORDE
Publishing, inc.

Dageforde Publishing, Inc.
122 South 29th Street
Lincoln, Nebraska 68510
Ph: (402) 475-1123; FAX: (402) 475-1176
email: info@dageforde.com
Visit our website: www.dageforde.com

Printed in the United States of America
10   9   8   7   6   5   4   3   2   1

For B.L.U.

Contents

Introduction

The courageous lawmen who helped tame the wild and woolly West of the 19th Century share a place of honor in the history of America. They came in all sizes, shapes, and degrees of law enforcement. Some had motives that were suspect. Men like Wyatt, Virgil, and Morgan Earp have left over a century of suspicion as to how honorable their motives were on a blustery October 1881 afternoon in Tombstone, Arizona, when they gunned down Tom and Frank McLowry and Billy Clanton near the O.K. Corral.

Some men, like Frank M. Canton, seemed to dance recklessly on the thin line that separated lawmen from outlaws. Canton worked as range detective for a time, but then, using the name Joe Horner, dropped out of sight between 1871 and 1878. He was jailed for bank robbery in Comanche, Texas. Moving to Wyoming, he again worked as a cattle detective and was sheriff of Johnson County. In that position, he was accused of the ambush murder of two ranchers. With things too hot for him in Wyoming, Canton eventually held deputy U.S. marshal positions in Oklahoma and Alaska. Toward the end of his days, he was the adjutant general of the Oklahoma National Guard. He died in Oklahoma during 1927.

Mysterious Dave Mather baffled folks, too. Accused at various times of horse stealing, and bank and train robbery, Mather was run out of Fort Worth, Texas, because he stole a gold chain and ring from a woman. In Kansas, he held the law offices of assistant marshal, deputy sheriff, and city marshal. It was while Mather was

1

a deputy sheriff in Ford County that he sought out an enemy; a man named Tom Nixon. When Mather spotted him, he called out to Nixon, pulled his Colt .42, and shot him four times, dead. Mather admitted, "I ought to have killed him six months ago." Mather moved on and was charged with murder in a shooting fray over a card game. Mather jumped bail. What happened to Mysterious Dave after that? That's—yes—a mystery.

And what about Sheriff Patrick Floyd Garrett's role in blasting the notorious Billy the Kid from ambush? Or how about Henry Newton Brown, who rode with Billy the Kid? Brown, a native of Rolla, Missouri, and three-time city marshal of Caldwell, Kansas, put away his badge one Wednesday morning in 1884, rode over to Medicine Lodge and robbed the Medicine Valley Bank. Local folks didn't take kindly to this. They tried to lynch Brown, but shot him to death instead.

"In the line of duty" took new meaning for City Marshal C.M. Taylor of Baxter Springs, Kansas, during the summer of 1872. Marshal Taylor, just doing his duty, sought out Baxter Springs mayor, J.R. Boyd. Boyd had argued with a local businessman named Smith. When Boyd ran out of words, he began beating Smith around the head. Smith was upset, detested this sort of behavior, especially when it was exacted on his head. He demanded satisfaction in the form of swearing out a complaint. Marshal Taylor carried the warrant for assault to Mayor Boyd. Boyd, his blood still boiling over the Smith affair, promptly took out his wrath on the marshal. He shot Taylor. Killed him.

Down in El Paso, Texas, City Constable John Henry Selman learned early that it was foolish to take chances with those living outside the law. As a matter of fact, Selman had been an outlaw for a time and had firsthand knowledge about how treacherous outlaws could be. Selman made a living for a while as a saloon keeper and then turned to selling John Deere farm equipment. In 1894, while preserving the peace in El Paso, Selman found gunfighter John Wesley Hardin in the Acme Saloon and opened fire. Hardin, hit in the back of the head, died. Strangely, on Easter Sunday four years later, the drunken Selman was shot to death outside the Wigwam Saloon by U.S. Marshal George Scarborough. Selman took four bullets without firing a shot from his .45 Colt Single Action Army revolver. And when Selman was down, Scarborough pumped three more shots in the body as Selman lay on the ground. There was bad blood between the two men over a game of cards.

Many lawmen spent their entire lives upholding the law—most of the time. Henry Andrew Thomas, better known as Heck Thomas, was born in Georgia, near Atlanta, a decade before the Civil War began. He worked in many capacities, always upholding the law in one way or the other. Thomas was appointed deputy U.S. marshal and worked out of Fort Smith, Arkansas, for many years. It was in this capacity, during 1886, that he went after the notorious bank robber Bill Doolin. In a nighttime ambush, Thomas blasted Doolin from the saddle with his L.C. Smith 12-gauge shotgun. The blast from Thomas' double-barreled shotgun—and probably those of his deputies—left twenty-one buckshot holes in Doolin.

Thomas later told how it was, explaining that Doolin was coming down the lane, firing first a big Winchester, then going to his pistol. "About this time," Marshal Thomas related, "I got the shotgun to work and the fight was over."

Thomas finished his last seven years in law enforcement in Lawton, Oklahoma. He was let go when his health failed. Three years later, in 1912, he died in Lawton.

And another honest lawman was Edward J. Masterson, the older brother of the more famous Bat Masterson. Born in Canada in 1852, Ed wound up in Kansas in the 1870s and, by April, 1878, was doing a tolerable job maintaining peace as City Marshal of Dodge City. But then the mysterious, the unknown, intervened.

While making the rounds with policeman Nat Haywood, the two entered Josh Webb's Lady Gay Saloon and spotted a drunken cowboy wearing a revolver in a shoulder holster. There was a city ordinance against wearing firearms. But it was not a problem; the cowboy surrendered it and Masterson turned it over to the cowboy's trail boss.

A short time later, when Masterson and Haywood began their rounds again, they stepped into the night and onto the front porch of the Lady Gay and were followed closely by the drunken cowboy and his boss. There was a movement to unholster a gun, a scuffle, a blast from the muzzle of a pistol. Another blast. Three more explosions. And then deadly quiet mixed with the acrid smell of gun smoke.

Ed Masterson emerged from all this, stepped into the street, headed across the railroad tracks and aimed at the kerosene light coming from Hoover's Saloon. There was a flicker of flame coming from Masterson's coat. And then he was in front of Hoover's. Bartender George Hinkel was on the porch, waiting for Masterson now. Masterson collapsed at his feet. Hinkel sat down and cradled the fallen lawmen's head.

"George, I'm shot," Masterson said, matter-of-factly. The twenty-five-year-old lawman died forty minutes later. His killer, it was found later, had fallen off a horse a few weeks earlier. He hit his head. He hadn't been quite right since. Things sometimes happened that way to lawmen—and cowboys—in the West.

As for weapons, these lawmen used what was available. The Civil War had seen to it that practically every frontier male and most of the women, often for secondary reasons, knew how to handle a gun of some kind. Shotguns and rifles were practical around the homestead, whether it be for protecting cattle from wolves and coyotes, hunting deer, or driving cattle out of cropland. And for a cowboy living in the open several months of each year, a handgun was often essential.

Many of the Civil War veterans, North and South, stepped into civilian life with the Colt Navy .36 caliber, a nice, lightweight pistol, but without the hitting power of the larger, heavier Remington New Model Army .44. Both weapons were six-shot percussion pistols. Each chamber had to be loaded with powder, a patch, a ball, and a percussion cap. But if these weapons were dangerous

4

to those being shot at, they were also dangerous for the shooter. In too many cases, wet powder failed to explode. Many a gunfighter experienced that horrible feeling when the hammer fell on a cap and no explosion came from the pistol. The experience was seldom repeated. In even more serious cases, all the chambers of the percussion pistols fired at once, often disintegrating the pistol—and the hand of the gunman. The 1860 Colt .44 was this type, also.

After the Civil War, the first metallic-cartridge revolvers appeared. The Army adopted the Colt Peacemaker .45 and civilians could get it through the mail for under $20. Colt produced several styles of this .45 caliber, single-action revolver. Over 350,000 of them were produced by the Colt's Patent Fire Arms Manufacturing Company in Hartford, Connecticut. Smith & Wesson, Remington, and several English firms continued to produce competition for Colt.

Besides the handguns, there were the various Winchester rifles that followed the 1860 Henry .44 Repeating Rifle. The lever action feature was adopted by Winchester in a .44 caliber weapon that would hold from 14 to 18 rounds (according to whether it was the shorter carbine or not). The Winchester carbines were introduced in 1866. It would be several years later, in 1873, before the Winchester .44-.40 came onto the market. It became the most popular rifle in the Old West. And, of course, the shotgun was used by various lawmen and outlaws.

But this book deals with two lawman. One, under normal circumstances, preferred not to use such weapons. His name was Bear River Tom Smith and his weapons were his fists. As Chief of Police, Smith set out to bring civilization to frontier Kansas. To do that, he had to tame the lawless cowboys and rowdies that arrived with the Texas cattle herds. His other duty was to preserve civilization for the farmers and merchants that came from the East. As part of the plan to do that, it was Chief of Police Smith's job to forbid the carrying of guns in the city limits of the frontier outpost called the West's first cow town, Abilene, Kansas.

The year after Chief Tom Smith tamed Abilene with his fists, he was succeeded by James Butler Hickok. Hickok was not a two-fisted law enforcement officer, but a two-gun law enforcement officer known throughout the West as Wild Bill. Their styles of law enforcement were different. Both were brave, courageous law officers, but Hickok's smoking guns sometimes dealt justice carelessly—and too quickly. Smith, on the other hand, may have been too hesitant whenever it came time to carry out the letter of the law.

Smith, his fists ready to strike like a rattlesnake, quickly gained the respect of violators of the laws set forth in Abilene. Hickok's ace-in-the-hole seems to have been fear, the fear that Hickok's lightning draw would deal death to lawbreakers—and in Hickok's case, anyone else who got in the way.

Like Chief Smith, Hickok had experience dealing with the hard men that peopled the frontier. Hickok's reputation preceded him; Smith's reputation developed over the weeks and months he served as the Chief of Police of Abilene, Kansas.

The Smith-Hickok Years

1870

- An Ellsworth, Kansas, dance house shoot-out leaves Fanny Collins dead and Nettie Baldwin near death. (January)
- John D. Rockefeller forms the Standard Oil Company into a monopoly. (January)
- Montana's Baker Massacre; estimated 170 Piegan Indians slaughtered (February)
- Construction begins on the Northern Pacific Railroad (February)
- Utah Territory grants full suffrage to women (February)
- Fifteenth Amendment to the US Constitution ratified (March)
- Six-in-hand California stagecoach driver Charlie Pankhurst retires (*He* was a fifty-eight-year-old *she*.)
- Sixteen-year-old gambler Luke Short, "The Undertaker's Friend," leaves his Texas home for good
- Thomas James Smith hired as Abilene chief of police (June)
- US population is 38,558,371 (June)
- US Department of Justice created (June)
- Dickinson County population doubles to over 3,000; 2/3rds farmers
- Confederate General Robert E. Lee dies (October)
- Bear River Tom Smith is murdered (November)

1871

- Future President Grover Cleveland becomes sheriff of Erie County, New York (January)
- First gunfight in Wichita, Kansas; several die (March)
- An Apache war breaks out in Arizona (April)
- James Butler Hickok hired as Abilene's chief of police (April)
- Thomas Masterson and sons, Bat, Jim, and Ed, move to Sedgwick County, Kansas (June)
- Kiowa Satanta sentenced to death for the Warren Massacre (July)
- Gunfighter John Wesley Hardin killed Bideno in Kansas (July)
- "Newton's General Massacre" leaves nine dead or wounded (August)
- Great Chicago Fire kills estimated 300 (October)
- Quanah Parker became headman of the Kwahadi Comanches
- Brigham Young and other Morman leaders accused of polygamy (October)
- Peshtigo, Wisconsin fire kills 800 (October)
- Rioting breaks out against Chinese in Los Angeles; 22 killed (October)
- President Ulysses S. Grant issues proclamation against Ku Klux Klan (October)
- Henry M. Stanley "discovers" Dr. David Livingstone (November)
- Wild Bill Hickok discharged by Abilene city council (December)

THOMAS JAMES SMITH
1870

*Abilene Marshal Thomas J. Smith tried to control
outlaws with fists, rather than guns.*
(photo courtesy Dickinson County Historical Library)

*In years to come there will be those who will look
back to the days when it required brave hearts and
strong hands to put down barbarism in this new
country and among the names of the bravest and the
truest none will be more gratefully remembered than
that of THOMAS JAMES SMITH, the faithful
officer and true friend of Abilene.*

—The Abilene *Chronicle*,
November 3, 1870

1875 Abilene. The Abilene known to Smith and Hickok looked something like this. (photo courtesy Dickinson County Historical Society)

The Worst Town in America

In the spring of 1870, Abilene's reputation, in the eyes of many, was one of wickedness, brutality, and cruelty. In the words of one observer, it was "the worst town in America, the first of its cattle kind (Jameson, p. 32-33)." Trouble wrought by herds of Texas cattle spread over the frontier town. It was a sin city. The streets weren't safe. Bullets flew at any hour. There were loose women and there were loose morals. There were rumors of murder and there was murder.

Since the Texans began coming in August and September 1867, life had changed drastically in Abilene. Where ramshackle, dirt-roofed cabins had stood, there were now buildings made of wood planks. And not only the shelters had changed, but the moral bearing of the community was altered.

As a sin city, Abilene was a nest of misfits, especially when the cattle herds from Texas arrived in town. The cowboys were wild when they reached Abilene. Everything was done to excess. Cowboys didn't drink; they got roaring drunk. They didn't walk the streets; they reeled and staggered. They didn't converse on the streets; they screamed and shouted. They didn't dine at local eating houses; they ate like pigs at a trough. They didn't wear their guns; they unholstered them and blasted everything in sight. They didn't court local girls; they grabbed the first prostitute they found. It was uncivilized. And the decent people that called Abilene home wanted it stopped!

The great cattle herds and the cowboys that drove them were the cause. They came up from Texas for the same reason Easterners came to Abilene—money. During the Civil War, the Confederate State of Texas was not hard hit by the war and came through the four years relatively unscathed. The members of the Texas soldier's family that stayed home herded cattle and made sure the calves were branded. Many of the ranchers were short-handed and cattle often strayed over large areas. Energetic young men and boys hunted Longhorns over great distances, pulling together large, well-fed herds off grassy plains that once fed great herds of grazing buffalo.

Following the war, it was only a matter of time until Texans learned of the high price of cattle in the Eastern United States. Long trail drives to the railroads that were crossing the West was the next factor. And soon, Joseph G. McCoy's stockyards at Abilene became the destination of nearly every herd leaving Texas. Driving those herds were men set on making a living and seeing some other part of the country than where they had grown up.

These cowboys, many young and restless, had wound their way from Texas to Abilene, following the twisting, turning trail, skipping from stream to stream. Their young minds were often filled with visions of what it would be when they reached trail's end. For many, it was the first time they'd been away from home, the first chance they'd had to sow their wild oats. Drawn up around the campfire at night, they exchanged stories and heard the old timers—someone who'd been on a drive before—talk about the way it was in Abilene. The beer, in their minds, was often colder; the women more beautiful. Always, it was the same. Their imaginations improved reality.

The best known cattle trail, the one Texas cowboys and the Longhorn steers followed, was the trail established by old Jesse Chisholm. Chisholm, of Scottish-Cherokee blood, was active as a guide and scout for the U.S. Army as early as the 1830s. He dealt with the Caddo, Delaware, Shawnee, Comanche, Wichita, and other tribes right up to the Civil War. Then he traded with both

Confederate and Union forces. It was the grassy, well-watered Civil War trading route through Oklahoma with a starting point in San Antonio, Texas, and an ending point in Abilene, Kansas, that he gave his name to—the Chisholm Trail.

These trail drives could be painfully dull and tiring, and they could test the soul of a man. Hardships came in many forms. The weather—too dry or too wet—could turn a cattle drive into disaster. There were streams—or raging rivers—to cross. A relatively safe ford might turn bad because of quicksand. Horses and cattle ran for little reason, turning peaceful nights into racing nightmares. Rustlers and Indian tribes were always a threat to the large herds.

And if a young cowboy survived all of that, despite 18 hours a day in the saddle, a confrontation between a rattlesnake and a spooked horse could upend the cowboy. If he hit the ground head first, or landed on a rock, it could be a fatal—and final— adventure.

One cowboy, George Duffield, drove a herd north from Texas in 1866. He kept a diary of his experiences. Excerpts follow:

Upset our wagon in River & lost Many of our cooking utensils. —was on my Horse the whole night & it raining hard one of our party Drowned to day Horses all give out & Men refused to do anything not having had a bite to eat for 60 hours Indians very troublesome We Hauled cattle out of the Mud with oxen half the day Hands all Growling & Swearing Sick & discouraged am in a Hel of a fix I had a sick headache bad Flies was worse than I ever saw them Found a Human skeleton on the Prairie to day (Duffield, pp. 243-262)

If Texas cowboys survived the grueling trip to Abilene, if they dodged all the pitfalls, all the bad luck that could have brought them down, then they celebrated. And the fact that they survived made them feel even more invincible. They were ready for anything. And figured they'd survive it.

After the Civil War, Abilene was just west of Kansas farm-lands. It was an ideal location for Springfield, Illinois, cattle broker Joseph McCoy. He had learned cattle brokering with his brothers and the firm of William K. McCoy and Brothers. With knowledge gained in conversations with his friends, Charles F. Gross and W.W. Sugg, plans for getting Texas cattle north took shape (Dykstra, p. 17).[1] Through deals with railroads, cattlemen, and stockyards, McCoy turned Abilene into the first cow town. He wrote later, "Abilene was selected because the country was en-tirely unsettled, well watered, excellent grass, and nearly the en-tire area of country was adapted to holding cattle. And it was the farthest point east at which a good depot for cattle business could have been made."

There was little question about it; the town was everything a cattleman needed. In the midst of oceans of tall grass, it was an ideal place to fatten cattle before shipping to the Eastern stock-yards. Besides the good water nearby, Fort Riley, just east up the Kansas Pacific Railroad, was close enough to protect everyone from the Indian disturbances like those in Colorado, Oklahoma, Wyoming, and the Dakotas. It was an ideal place to drive cattle to and to ship cattle from.

McCoy's Great Western Stockyards stood just east of Abilene at the end of Texas Street. There was nothing fancy about the stockyards. They were built of railroad ties that McCoy had talked the railroad into supplying. Some lumber came by rail from Hanni-bal, Missouri. There was hardwood from Lanape, Kansas.

The railroad built transfer and feed yards at Leavenworth. Both the railroad and McCoy had invested in the project. Esti-mates put McCoy's part in the venture at $35,000. His brother James Parkinson McCoy shared in the building ("Two City Mar-shals," p. 28).

The cattle drovers mostly stayed at the eighty-room Drover's Cottage. It stood about a quarter of a mile from the Great Western Stockyards Office and loading and feeding pens. The Drover's Cottage on Texas Street was a popular place that served cold drinks and hot beef steaks. It was an elegant establishment, one that drew all sorts of folks. One Abilene observer remembered: "On its lordly porch strayed or sat lordly Texan drovers, eastern city cattle buyers and commission agents, all exhaling an air of circumbient substantiality (Henry, S., p. 62)."

After he thought about it for a moment, he added, "Not to be omitted from this parade were at times leading saloonkeepers, gamblers and individuals known to have killed a white man."

McCoy had begun the building as a large, three-story hotel. He spent $15,000 in building the 40 X 50 foot building. That included the furnishings.

This drawing of an Abilene dance hall during cowboy days appeared in Joseph McCoy's *Historic Sketches of the Cattle Trade, 1874.*

It was a remarkable sight, rising out of the Kansas plains like it did. Inside, there was a dining room where a hungry man could order that delicious beefsteak. From the billiard parlor came the restful clack of pool balls striking each other and racing around the beautiful wood, slate, and green cloth-covered billiard tables. The saloon always seemed to be busy, but with a more reserved clientele than one found at the Texas Street saloons on the opposite side of the tracks. Out back, there was a carriage house.

There was a great deal of style in everything about the hotel. The hotel rooms were all elaborately furnished. The saloon had the look of a private club. Those that stayed there all seemed to be more reserved than the typical visitor to Abilene.

Between 1869 and 1870, the hotel was sold three times. In the fall of 1870, Moses B. George, a Texas cattle buyer bought and enlarged the Drover's Cottage. For most of 1870, the Drover's Cottage was under the direction—and ownership of—Colonel and Mrs. James W. Gore, expert managers from St. Louis (Brown & Schmitt, p. 64). By the spring of 1871, the Drover's Cottage was 70 X 90 feet with nearly one hundred rooms. It had started with over forty rooms. By the spring of 1871, the stable housed fifty carriages and one hundred horses (Dykstra, p. 99).

Visitors to Abilene were always struck by the noises of the cow town. A relatively slow, quiet horseback ride across the windswept prairies was met in Abilene with bawling herds of cattle. Cowboys at the stockyards shouted and cursed, snapping bull whips, moving the nervous cattle into pens, onto ten-ton scales and eventually into waiting cattle cars. It was a very confusing scene to a visitor not familiar with the goings on.

The frantic cowpunchers knew their work. The popping whips, the whistling ropes and the shouts and curses all served the purpose of getting the cattle onto the trains. Once that was done, their jobs were done. This noisy cowboy activity could ready forty carloads of cattle in two hours, according to one observer.

Abilene residents got used to it, but visitors were often amazed at the amount of traffic on Abilene's dirt streets. The stockyards and Texas Street were either six inches deep in dust, or a foot deep in mud. There didn't seem to be any in between. And when there was a long spell between rains, a cloud of dust hung over the stockyards and sometimes the town. It just hung there, waiting for rain to settle it or wind to blow it to Missouri. There just wasn't any time in the spring and summer that people in Abilene weren't very much aware of the Texas cattle.

Some estimate that 160,000 head of cattle were driven up from Texas during 1869, the year before Marshal Tom Smith arrived on the scene. One Abilene resident figured that they were coming so fast in 1870 that it took 1,000 cattle cars a month to keep up a steady flow of shipping. Others claimed that the total herd from Texas in 1870 was 300,000 head.

As for how much a Texas rancher could make on these drives, M.A. Withers drove a herd to Abilene in 1868. He claimed he drove 600 Longhorn steers north. He had purchased the steers for $8 to $10 a head. It cost him $4 a head to drive them to Abilene. His profit was $9,000. The next year, James F. Ellison made $9,000 on 750 steers. As the years passed, drovers learned how to improve their profits (Dary, *Cowboy Culture*, p. 209).

On arrival in Abilene, the cowboys picked up their pay—usually $30 or $40 a month, more if they owned their own horses. Then it was time to turn their fantasies into reality. They swarmed over the little town, washed tubsful of dirt from their bodies, got their hair cut and bought clothes that weren't stiff with sweat and dirt.

"Dressed in gala attire," one visitor noted, "they wore high-heeled boots with large clanking spurs of various hues, shirts that bloused freely with no hint of suspenders, large colored handkerchiefs knotted loosely around their necks and large-brimmed Stetson hats. Some showed the influence of their Spanish neighbors and wore large brightly colored sashes (Stratton, p. 218)."

Cowboys from Mexico were easily spotted with their big sombreros. They often wore colorful clothing and shiny, jangling rowled spurs with silver conchs. Most spoke passable English and knew cattle and how to herd them. Even their saddles, bridles, and other horse gear had a special style.

Once a cowboy got all spruced up, then it was time to take over Texas Street. With pockets full of money, these young Texans violated every town law, ever law of decency, and every law of man.

Even a respectable, law-abiding citizen of Abilene who tried crossing the street risked life and limb. If he wasn't careful, some cowboy might ride a horse down Texas Street as fast as he could spur
him on, dust and dirt clods flying. And in the process, the rambunctious cowboy might pull his pistol and blast away at anything
that moved. If the careless cowboy didn't have that kind of ten-
dency, then there were thirty-two places where he could buy crazy
in a bottle and then shoot up the town without guilt clouding his
judgment. Hell came to Abilene to roost when the cowboys turned
loose.

If that wasn't enough excitement, gaming houses were full of
outlaws, gamblers, and flim-flam men who would gladly replace
some of the cowboy's boredom with a game of "chance." Who was
responsible for all this? None other than Illinoisan Joseph G. Mc-
Coy. He arrived in Kansas wearing "heavy boots, short topcoat,
black slouch hat" and a "goatee that hid a weak chin lending age to
his twenty-nine years (Dykstra, p. 99)."

Joseph G. McCoy saw Abilene grow from a few cabins to a rip-
roaring cow town. As a matter of fact, McCoy holds the title of
"the father of the cow town." He authored a book, *Historic Sketches
of the Cattle Trade of the West and Southwest* about those Abilene
and Kansas days. He wrote: "Many strangers congregate, there are
always to be found a number of bad characters, both male and female; of the very worst class in the universe, such as have fallen below the level of the lowest type of the brute creation. Men who live
a soulless, aimless life, dependent upon the turn of a card for the
means of living (Jameson, p. 22)."

Amidst all of this, the "working girls" were bent on plying their
trade among these lawless characters that this town with the biblical name attracted along with the cow trade in the 1860s and 70s.
These women painted themselves, slipped on their best corsets
and their fanciest dresses, and showed off their wares until one of
man's strongest urges separated him from his money for the thrill
of a few minutes on a tick mattress with one of these soiled doves.

All these sorts were, in McCoy's estimation, "Beings without whom the world would be better, richer and more desirable (McCoy, p. 138)." It was the combination, then, of the cowboys and the characters living on the edge of the law that made Abilene an evil place during these cattle driving days.

Any attempt at calming this calamitous behavior, taming this lawless crowd, fell short. The merchants and settled citizens of Abilene looked high and low for help. They needed order in their town. None seemed to fit the bill. Any lawkeeper that Abilene hired during the late 1860s had to have rare qualities of character and demeanor. He had to be willing to risk life and limb by simply walking the streets. The good people of Abilene wanted some sort of sanity in regard to gun control. Was there a man brave enough to attempt to disarm a drunken cowboy—especially when the cowboy had ten, or twenty, or thirty armed friends to back him up? To many, it seemed a hopeless situation.

Men were hired, good men. Abilene hired constables from March of 1867, but these cowboys and the crowd there to greet them were too many. In the numbers they were coming, it was too much to ask an ordinary man to control. It was too much to ask several ordinary men to control. The numbers were simply too great, too overwhelming. There were several good men that might bring civilization to Abilene, but they were not right for such a job. As a matter of fact, T.C. Henry wrote later, "The first two seasons no effort was made to control the disorder and suppress the brazen lawlessness of the rough element gathered here [Abilene] ("Two City Marshals," p. 138)." Most law enforcement officials simply did not see the special problems created by the Texas cattlemen as their problem.

Joseph G. McCoy, the man who brought Texas cattle and Texas cowboys to Abilene, saw this lawlessness arrive, grow, prosper, and overwhelm the community. It was his idea that a town like this needed a special breed of man. He wrote, "No quiet turned man could or would care to take the office of marshal, which jeopardized his life; hence the necessity of employing a desperado, one who feared nothing, and would as soon shoot an offending subject as to look at him (McCoy, p. 139)."

So there was the formula, according to a man who lived in Abilene nearly from the beginning. You could not hire a "quiet turned man." What Abilene needed was "a desperado," and a fearless one to boot. A gunfighter who would shoot first and ask questions later. One that would maintain law and order by breaking the law. One that would turn Abilene's streets into streets of blood.

The citizens of Abilene moved closer to solving their peacekeeping problems when they incorporated the city. Probate Judge Cyrus Kilgore ordered the incorporation on September 3, 1869, after forty-three Abilene residents had signed the order. Abilene was incorporated as a third class city and a board of trustees was appointed until an election could be held.

As a part of the incorporation, Dickinson County appointed Theodore C. Henry to the position of mayor of Abilene. Henry, from New York, had tried his hand at growing cotton in Alabama. He abandoned that in favor of the study of law. It was while studying in the law office of Joseph McCoy's attorney that Henry was convinced by McCoy that Kansas was the land of opportunity. After a few months in Kansas, Henry, bought into a real estate office with James B. Shane, an ex-Union Army officer from Kentucky (Dykstra, p. 294-295).[2] [Shane and Henry, Real Estate Brokers had a secret partner, "probably S.A. Burroughs," county attorney during 1871-72. (McCoy, p.137)] Henry and Shane had every reason to see Abilene tamed and kept that way so that men and home-building women might settle there, free from the fear of the typical frontier community. Mayor Theodore C. Henry began looking for a solution to the lawlessness (Dykstra, p. 295).

The County of Dickinson was already in business. Tom Sheran [Sherran], in addition to operating a grocery store, was the sheriff of Dickinson County, but he couldn't deal with Abilene's trouble. He was head of the county's executive branch. He was serving the county as an executive officer, not as a gun fighting, law enforcement officer. (Sheran was also one of the first trustees of Abilene.

The others appointed during 1869 were Henry's partner, James B. Shane, Tim Hersey and Joseph McCoy. In the spring of 1870, Hersey and McCoy were replaced by real estate man C.H. Lebold and Dr. H.C. Brown. Lebold and his partner, Jacob Augustine, had arrived in the fall of 1869 and purchased the Abilene town site from C.H. Thompson and Joseph McCoy for $3,000. Lebold and Augustine formed the National Union Land Office. Washburne Fancher, the young school master, was secretary of the board.)

Sheriff Sheran soon turned in his badge. His deputy, a young Canadian named James H. McDonald, took over. McDonald, about twenty-one years old, was tall and had a fair complexion. He too did not last long in that position (Cushman, p. 248-250).

The trustees had the right ideas. They knew what they wanted for their town. They knew that they had to bring it under control. Licensing was one way of bringing control. They passed laws to license saloons and houses of prostitution. They let it be known by posting signs around town that they planned to take control of Abilene.

But when signs explaining Abilene town ordinances were posted, they were torn down. "No shooting" signs were riddled with bullets. The game in Abilene was to defy law and order, make a mockery of it, laugh at it.

When law-abiding townsmen attempted to build a small stone jail to house lawbreakers, it was torn down. Mayor Henry, reaching frustration, did all he could. He hired guards to watch the new jail construction night and day. And when the jail was finally finished—under heavy guard, the town relaxed. The guards went home. The job was done.

But then one night, the Texans came to town to retrieve one of their cooks who had been jailed. The tough Texans ran off the guards who watched over the jail when there were prisoners. Then they shot the lock off the door and galloped up and down the streets of Abilene emptying their six-shooters into any post, sign, or window that struck their fancy. And then, amid all the pistols banging away and the whooping and hollering, they raced down the streets and out of town, back to their herd and camp.

Terrified townsmen were furious. They wouldn't tolerate such lawlessness, even if it meant giving up the lucrative trade that the cowboys and cattle buyers brought to Abilene. A group of towns-men armed themselves, harnessed their horses, hitched them to wagons, and rode after the culprits. The surprised cowboys hadn't witnessed this kind of reaction before. (Even the townsmen sur-prised themselves.)

Abilene's irate citizens arrested several cowboys, but never did find the leader of the jailbreakers or the fugitive cook. After this, for a time, the trustees became the object of the wrath of some of the citizenry. Something had to be done. Abilene was not a fit place to raise a family with this type thing going on during cattle season. What were they to do? Should they cower in their homes all summer? Or retreat to the relative sanity of Kansas City?

Mayor Henry's brother, Stuart Henry, reflecting on his bro-ther's situation several years later, probably summed it up best when he wrote, "My brother became mayor of the worst town in America, the first of its cattle kind, and by this time known as such in the nation (Jameson, p. 32-33)."

But the problem that Mayor Henry had to deal with was how to put down that reputation. How did he go about turning a law-less town into a civilized town? How did he overcome what cat-tle—and time—had brought to Abilene?

Town Tamer

There were all sorts of reasons why reasonable people left the relative calm of America's settled farms, safe towns, and civilized cities for the uncertainty of the frontier. Railroad promoters encouraged settlement in the West so that they could sell off the land the government had given them in exchange for laying railroad tracks from coast to coast. Emigration societies were in the business of moving people and people wanted to move. State politicians had everything to gain with population increases to their territories and states. Real estate agents were eager to sell real estate. All these reasons and many assorted others contributed to the settlement of towns like Abilene during the last half of the 19th Century.

Times and the population had certainly changed in Abilene since 1867 when Joseph McCoy noted that it was a "small, dead place" with a dozen huts made of logs. They were low and small, "rude affairs," complete with dirt roofs (McCoy, p. 44). Someone called it a pitiful little town.

There was a stone relay house just across Mud Creek on the town's west edge. Timothy Hersey had built a cabin of hewn logs, then added the stone stable covered with a dirt roof. It was Hersey's wife, Elizabeth, that thumbed her Bible open to Luke and found the name Abilene. The name has since taken on the meaning of "City of the Plains (Henry, S., p. 20)."

Hersey's log cabin served the Butterfield Overland Dispatch as Station Number Two on the line established between Atchison and Denver. The relay house had been there since 1865 and was the first relay station west of Fort Riley. All of this represented the progress made since the town was laid out on C.H. Thompson's land in 1860 (McCoy, p. 203-204).

Still it wasn't much of a town. McCoy recalled a story making the rounds. It seems a Texas drover on his first trip north to Abilene rode into town one morning. He reined his horse to a halt right in the middle of town and asked how far and in what direction was Abilene?

The puzzled drover was told he was in Abilene. This was it. The Texan shook his head, then said sincerely, "Now, look here, stranger, you don't mean this here little scatterin' trick is Abilene."

It was, the stranger answered.

Shaking his head and smiling, the drover looked around and said, "Well, I'll swar I never seed such a little town have such a mighty big name (Stratton, p. 206)."

Back in 1860, no one in Kansas was much concerned about Texas cattle. The next year, when Kansas became a state, the first state legislature passed laws forbidding the Texas Longhorns from coming north into Kansas during the warm part of the year. One woman recalled, "Texas cattle could not come into the state unless they were dipped to kill the ticks on them (McCoy, p. 202-204)." The problem was tick fever or piroplasmosis. For some reason, Texas Longhorns weren't bothered by the ticks. But as cowboys pushed the cattle north, the ticks fell from the Longhorns and were eventually picked up by herds of northern cattle that were not immune to the tick. The result was that northerners wanted nothing to do with Texas cattle. And certainly did not want them driven across the pastures where their susceptible cattle grazed.

But money has a way of tearing down many barriers. There was money to be made in Texas cattle. Ticks or not. By 1867, folks in Kansas realized that Texas cattle at Kansas railheads would generate that money. In 1867, the Kansas legislature demonstrated that they understood basic economics as well. Previously, they'd banned Texas cattle. They now modified their Texas Longhorn quarantine with the Act for the Protection of Stock from Disease. They gave their approval to bringing the infected Longhorns to Kansas, but only if they were kept west of the sixth principal meridian and south of a line drawn through the center of the state.

Then came the cows, the steers, and the bulls from Texas. Almost overnight, amazing things happened to Abilene. It became a cow town. One day it was a lonely collection of log cabins on the Kansas prairie, a railroad track running past it. And then, seemingly overnight, it was a great shipping center for cattle.

To advertise all of this and demonstrate the shipping technique, Joseph McCoy invited beef packers, cattle dealers, railroad officials, and their wives to Abilene in September 1867. Large tents were raised and the guests enjoyed food prepared by Mrs. Tim Hersey and other Abilene women.

Abilene's and McCoy's guests watched the cattle being weighed and loaded, then settled back for wine and speeches which lasted into the early morning. McCoy wrote, "Before the sun had mounted high in the heavens on the following day, the iron horse was darting down the Kaw Valley with the first train load of cattle that ever passed over the Kansas Pacific Railroad."

So, in a grand fashion, Abilene's citizens and Mr. McCoy had launched the Texas cattle trade in Kansas. But cattlemen and those connected with the trade were not the only ones who benefited from the Texas trade. Farmers also did well in Dickinson County. Dickinson County was typical upland plains. The Smoky Hill River flowed through the county, meandering its way from west to east in a shallow valley that averaged about a mile in width. Cottonwoods and river willows marked the streams and creeks and the early settlers sought them out. It was there that they planted vegetable gardens and patches of corn. And as cattle became the business of nearby Abilene, they brought their surpluses to town for sale.

Abilene became a collection point for farmers growing crops that they could sell to cattlemen and ship to eastern markets. McCoy noted, "The farmers of the county had a home demand, at high cash prices, for every bushel of grain, peck of vegetables, pound of butter, or dozen eggs that they could possibly produce; and still it was necessary to import many car-loads of these articles to supply the demand."

Joseph McCoy's interest in turning Texas Longhorns into a profit in the East had encouraged all this. A man who believed in advertising, McCoy wrote, "Perhaps no point or village of its size ever had been so thoroughly advertised, or had acquired such wide-spread fame." Because of that, McCoy would eventually note, "No point in the west of five times its resident population, did one-half the amount of business that was done at Abilene (Henry, S., p. 132)."

And in 1869, Abilene's problems had only just begun. Expansion was everywhere. The stockyards had just been enlarged to handle two or three herds of 1,000 head and a side track was lengthened so that more cattle could be prodded onto the cars and shipped East. Texas Street was cluttered with new, one-room frame buildings, set one or two feet above the ground and made of green lumber that warped and smelled of pine in the hot, summer heat.

Texas Street was laid out in peculiar fashion and was more an area than a street. Bounded on the north by the railroad, it lay along the railroad for two short blocks. Then, it turned south and ran for a block. Again, it ran east and west, one block in each direction.

And so, people around Abilene prospered, people in Abilene prospered, and Abilene prospered. Still, there was the problem: What about law enforcement? What to do with these go-to-hell manners of the young cowboys up from Texas with the herds?

Mayor Henry wrote later, "Growing cowboy insolence was exhibited in various ways—some ludicrous and laughable. The posted ordinances were viewed with a mixture of awe and curiosity at the outset, and gradually their significance and purpose was comprehended. Finally our failure to enforce order was contemptuously and concretely celebrated by the cowboy horsemen taking shots at the abortive fire-arms ordinance as they galloped by, until the city fathers themselves could not have traced the lineaments of this municipal offspring ("Two City Marshals," p. 528)." Henry said later, "Conditions grew steadily worse. Disdain for the law and its officers increased."

Reeling from the rowdy, hell-bent outlawry of the previous cattle season, on May 2, 1870, the town trustees created the office of marshal by city ordinance. They realized that they had to have a lawman on the job before the Texas herds arrived. It was time to be firm about law and order in Abilene, to take a stand. It was not enough that the city passed laws and set regulations. These laws had to be enforced. Abilene citizens needed to be firm and confront the Texans this summer.

The trustees continued adding new regulations. On May 12, 1870, the Abilene *Chronicle* set down the results of a trustee meeting. The marshal's duties included supervising the jail house, maintaining a record of all persons arrested, keeping a record of all persons confined, and controlling of the police force. The police were to keep order, to arrest and confine any person guilty of disorderly conduct or drunkenness. Those persons arrested were to be reported to a magistrate within twenty-four hours.

In addition, the marshal was to hold the position of street commissioner. This duty called for keeping the streets free of animate and inanimate hazards. It might include, as in Ellsworth, an ordinance that called for the street commissioner "to arrest swine found at large (Dykstra, p. 124)."

Laws were passed a few days later that prohibited firearms, fined prostitutes, and licensed saloons and gambling. The newspaper listed the new ordinances. Posters were printed and nailed at prominent places in town and on the roads leading into town. They were nice, substantial posters. They spelled out what would no longer be tolerated in Abilene. Things were going to change. Abilene would not put up with the lawlessness any longer. The city marshal would serve as captain of police. An assistant marshal might be hired and additional help would be referred to as policemen. Sometimes special policemen were hired for specific duties, such as keeping order at a particular place of business.

The new posters went up in Abilene and were promptly shot full of holes. And frustration begat frustration.

J.B. Edwards lived in Abilene during those early days, making a living sawing ice from the river and selling it to local merchants for six cents a pound (Cushman, p. 244). He observed the dangerous Texas cowboys and their six-shooting habits. He wrote, "If his fancy told him to shoot, he did so—into the air or at anything he saw. A plug hat would bring a volley from him at any time, drunk or sober (Brown, *Wondrous Times*, p. 117)."

These crazed cowboys came from long trail drives stretching hundreds of hard miles. Suffering from boredom, they visited the saloons, dance halls, a small theater, and brothels in search of a cure. Even though the cowboys were a thorn in his side, Joseph McCoy seemed to understand their plight. He wrote, "The life of the cow-boy in camp is routine and dull. His food is largely of the 'regulation' order, but a feast of vegetables he wants and must have, or scurvy would ensue. Onions and potatoes are his favorites, but any kind of vegetables will disappear in haste when put within his reach (McCoy, p. 137)."

Sympathetic with the condition of these herders, McCoy added, "They sleep on the ground, with a pair of blankets for bed and cover. No tent is used, scarcely any cooking utensils, and such a thing as a camp cook-stove is unknown. The warm water of the branch or the standing pool is drank; often it is yellow with alkali and other poisons."

McCoy concluded, "No wonder the cow-boy gets sallow and unhealthy, and deteriorates in manhood until often he becomes capable of any contemptible thing; no wonder he should become half-civilized only, and take to whisky with a love excelled scarcely by the barbarous Indian (McCoy, p. 138)."

No wonder he was ready to shoot up and, otherwise hurrah, any town he came to. And to go with all these other excuses, the cowboy of the 1860s and 1870s was barely a man at all, often just a little older than "wet-behind-the-ears." Most of them had no education at all. One young Texan recalled his days in school and how far he went: "Well, when I got so I could draw a cow and mark a few brands on the slate, I figured I was getting too smart to go to school (Forbis, p. 20)."

Down on Texas Street, the saloons brimmed with these smart cowboys. There were shootings and knifings, conduct that the citizens of Abilene cringed at. There was always the fear that this behavior would spill over into the civilized part of town. Some of the fear was needless, but it was that gnawing kind of fear of which men in a lawless society can never rid themselves. It was the kind of fear that often leads men to desperate measures. It was the kind of fear that sometimes led to lynch law. None in Abilene wanted that. They had no intention of replacing their fear with guilt. They needed law and order. Desperately.

The chore was getting someone to enforce the laws. None of the local applicants who were hired to do the job lasted through a payday. For a while, there was a vigilance committee, but even that old wild and woolly West standard failed to clean up Abilene. Even a plan to hire policemen from St. Louis fell short.

Mayor Henry remembered, "The chief of police of St. Louis was implored to send us a couple of men competent to run the town for us ("Two City Marshals," p. 529). Two soldiers trained by the St. Louis police force were going to solve Abilene's problem, take care of the little city's woes.

The two imported, blue-uniformed lawmen, probably tired of the mean streets of St. Louis, arrived in the late spring of 1870. When the Kansas Pacific's big steam engine and train chugged and huffed into Abilene with the St. Louis policemen aboard, Mayor Henry felt somewhat relieved. Perhaps now there would finally be law and order in Abilene. Perhaps now the fine citizens and neighboring farmers out from the East would send for their families and not fear for their lives as they attempted to conduct business in Abilene.

The St. Louis policemen stepped off the train and left their luggage with D.R. Gordon, the young man who was the rail station agent. The two walked directly to Texas Street, passing up Mayor Henry's home, to size things up for themselves.

Abilene was still a small town in the matter of rumors. There were very few surprises. Truth and fiction traveled equally quickly through the town. Certainly, something as vital and significant to the future of the Kansas community as Mayor Henry's plan had been discussed at the town board meeting. One of the trustees boasted about how things were going to change in Abilene—just as soon as the new policemen from St. Louis arrived.

The St. Louis visitors no doubt saw what young Stuart Henry, the Mayor's brother, noticed and wrote about later. Henry described Abilene: "The village was ragged in appearance, incomplete anywhere, altogether unlovely, with facilities sadly lacking (Henry, S., p. 93)."

The policemen would have also noticed that the cowboys in the saloons were "ragged in appearance" and "altogether unlovely." Any cowboy worth his salt would have to do something threatening in the face of these new Eastern policemen.

Still, some would argue, these were men who were familiar with the hard cases on the waterfront along the landing in St. Louis. They'd seen the riverboat gamblers that made their living on the Mississippi. They'd seen the drunkenness on the St. Louis riverfront. Murder and mayhem was a part of the reputation of that old river town. Certainly, St. Louis had its hard cases, too.

But these two St. Louis policemen found quickly that Abilene could be awful and Texas Street terrible. Some of the toughs at the saloons and gaming houses on Texas Street prepared a little reception for the visiting policemen. At each establishment they entered, the two bewildered policemen heard threats, were jostled and cursed. The newcomers felt unwelcome, unwanted in these crude, social confrontations. Texas Street, it was made clear to them, would be their hell—if they lived long enough to experience it. It was a sobering experience for the two men. Neither had been

treated so rudely before. They had no desire to face this sort of uncivilized behavior again. In their mind's eye, St. Louis improved
considerably after this look at Abilene.

Without bothering to report to Mayor Henry, the policemen
from St. Louis decided against taking the job. The last anyone saw
of them on Texas Street, they were beating a hasty retreat toward
the rail depot. As a matter of fact, they collected their luggage
from a puzzled D. R. Gordon and skedaddled on the midnight train
bound for the sanity and relative safety of the East and the St.
Louis waterfront. No one knows if they ever ventured into the
West again.

Prior to the arrival of the policemen-soldiers from St. Louis, a
quiet man, a strong, clean-shaven, polite man had arrived to in-
quire of the marshal's job. Word had swept over the plains that the
city of Abilene was looking for a lawman. He sought out the mayor
and offered his services.

Mayor T.C. Henry took one look at the man and made up his
mind. This man was too small, too quiet to be a successful lawman
in this rough and rowdy town. No amount of information was going to change the mayor's mind. Henry was polite, listening to every word that handsome man said. Henry heard about his
experiences at Kit Carson (Colorado) and Bear River (Wyoming).
Mayor Henry had to admit, he sounded as if he had ample experience. But still Henry could not get by this calm, peaceful man's actions. There were no two ways about it. Henry decided he was too
polite, too gentlemanly to tame Abilene.

Following the interview, Mayor Henry half-heartedly discussed him with the trustees. Everything that Mayor Henry said
about this applicant was negative. There was no point in discuss-
ing him any further. Besides, all the information they had was from
him. Finally, Henry and the trustees rejected the quiet man. They
couldn't hire him; they hardly knew him. They certainly did not
know him well enough to turn over their town to him. They decided to make their choice from "home talent ("Two City Marshals," p. 528)."

But that didn't work either. What Henry called "growing cow-boy insolence" was too much for local officers. Henry's blinds that protected his office windows were destroyed. Henry's real estate partner, James B. Shane, was threatened ("Two City Marshals,"p. 529). And just days ago, those twenty cowboys had stormed into town, torn open the new jail, retrieved their jailed cook, ordered businesses closed in Abilene, and blasted holes in windows and buildings on their way out of town. Their cook, who had been so bold as to shatter a street light with his pistol, shouldn't be in jail, the cowboys reasoned in their lawless minds. The peace officer, a man named Robbins, was the temporary town policeman at the time (Drago, p. 71).

The cowboys had torn open the jail and removed their cook. Then, to top it all off, the Texans vandalized the mayor's office and shot random holes in other buildings during their retreat. Surely, Henry and the trustees reasoned, this kind, soft-spoken man named Smith with the neatly trimmed mustache and auburn hair could never tame Abilene.

Besides, two policemen were coming out from St. Louis. They'd been trained there. They had military experience. They'd know how to handle trouble.

Henry told the quiet man that the trustees were doing him a favor by not hiring him. It was a tough, life-threatening job, Henry pointed out. Dangerous job. Could get him shot—even killed.

The quiet man took it all in stride. He understood, he told Mayor Henry. The calm, understanding man bade Abilene fare-well and grabbed a westbound train.

But after the arrival—and hurried departure—of the soldier-policemen, Mayor Henry was desperate. He needed help and could only look to Smith, the quiet man, the gentlemanly man from Colorado Territory. Certainly, Smith hadn't run the way the two policemen had. He might just be their lawman. Perhaps they were too hasty in dismissing him. But then, they had figured the St. Louis policemen would solve their problem. Yes, indeed, the quiet man from Colorado might just get the job done. And besides, as

Henry remembered over three decades later, "We hungered for someone who could do to others what was doing to us, and to do them first. Therefore, I wired Tom Smith to come ("Two City Marshals," p. 529)."

The new train depot in Abilene was built from cottonwood lumber and sat along the south side of the Kansas Pacific track a block or so away from the reconstructed calaboose. There was nothing but a plank platform to greet the trains prior to 1869. In that year, the railroad was given some town property and built a depot that was 12 X 14 "with a four-foot by six-foot passenger waiting room (Cushman, p. 244)."

Mayor lived just southeast of the train station in the first frame house built in Abilene. It was about a block west of the Drover's Cottage. Mayor walked quickly to the train depot and explained the predicament to stationmaster D.R. Gorden. This fellow that had been in Abilene for the law job, the quiet one, the trustees wanted him back.

Gorden and Henry worked up a message. It was a delicate situation. Henry had rejected the man; rejected him out of hand. Would he return? They would try to locate the soft-spoken lawman, Thomas James Smith. Maybe he would make them a good lawman after all. A fellow couldn't tell what made a good lawman. There were all kinds. Some tough. Some not. Some honest. Some not. They were just people, men trying to get along in the world. Besides, Abilene was desperate for somebody to enforce the law. Mayor Henry said later of Smith, "He was endorsed by a reputable citizen of Abilene, who knew him as the accredited leader of the famed Bear River riot, in Wyoming ("Two City Marshals," p. 528)."

Gorden opened the telegraph key and tapped out the inquiry. Mayor Henry paced back and forth across the 14 X 28 room. Soon, the dots and dashes brought an answer. The man Mayor Henry was looking for, Tom Smith, had interrupted his trip to Denver. He was in Ellis, Kansas, just west of Fort Hays.

Henry sent another telegram. Would Smith consider returning to Abilene to discuss the job of town marshal? Certainly. Smith indicated he'd catch the next eastbound train.

It was Saturday morning, June 4, 1870, (Miller & Snell, p. 415) when Smith stepped off the train in Abilene, the big locomotive huffing and wheezing smoke and steam into the warm air. He brushed off his clothes the best he could, separating himself from the dirt and coal dust that train rides stirred up.

For the last few miles, the train had passed through great herds of cattle. Smith realized now that the town was practically surrounded by cattle. The great herds milled quietly in the surrounding grassy fields, waiting their turn to be herded into the stockyards at the east edge of Abilene. They'd be punched onto a huge Fairbanks scale, twenty or thirty at a time, and weighed. Finally loaded onto a cattle car, they'd ride the cattle cars back East to the killing pens. It was the 400- to 600-mile trail drive and this process in Abilene that turned a steer worth $2, $3, or $4 in Texas into a $40 steer in Abilene. And, obviously, the crowded industrial cities in the eastern United States contributed to the price, too.

Now Smith was back. His horse, Silverheels, (Rosa, *They Called Him Wild Bill*, p. 177) rode in on the same train. Smith led him out of the car and carefully down a ramp. Smith checked the animal's legs, found no scrapes or skins and decided the train ride had gone well. The big gray looked all right. The saddle needed adjusting.

Mayor Henry remembered, "Smith reappeared at my office. I related briefly the story of our troubles, and intimated that he had better first look over the situation, for possibly he might not care to undertake the job ("Two City Marshals," p. 529)."

"Smith," Mayor Henry began, "I'll tell you what to do. I want you to know what you are in for. Things are pretty tough," Henry added, nodding.

"I'm afraid," Henry warned, "it's going to get out of hand in spite of all. I advise you to look around Texas Street today. Then come back and we can do a little figuring."

Henry recalled, "He smiled rather grimly, but without a word proceeded on my hint ("Two City Marshals," p. 529)."

Actually, what Henry really had in mind went unsaid. He was all for Smith looking over Texas Street, but Henry wanted to have a chance to look Smith over as well. Then, too, Henry remembered what happened to the policemen-soldiers from St. Louis. He didn't want to waste his time on someone who'd be back on the train headed for someplace more civilized than Abilene. Put bluntly, Mayor Henry was still not convinced that Tom Smith was his man.

Smith rode the length of the north side of the tracks and turned south, walking the horse carefully over the tracks and down a sort of alley between buildings and into Texas Street, headed east toward Cedar. The smell of fresh pine lumber was everywhere. He learned later that much of the pine had been shipped in from Hannibal, Missouri, and carpenters came out from the East and frantically threw up many of the saloons and buildings in Abilene. That had been both in the fall of 1868 and of 1869. The buildings, many lacking paint, grayed in the weather.

Smith passed the site of the jail and McInerney's Boot Shop. He reined Silverheels left at the corner and rode at an angle past the Alamo Saloon, then around the corner onto Texas again. (This was actually A Street, sometimes called Railroad Street. Others, however, called it Texas Street.) He rode relaxed, but straight in the saddle. His strong left hand held the reins loosely woven through his fingers, his right arm hanging at his side. His head was straight ahead, but his eyes took it all in. Soon it would be Saturday night. He'd seen tough towns before. He'd seen tough towns on Saturday night before. Abilene didn't seem any tougher to him than those others, Saturday night or not.

At the mayor's office, Mayor Henry recalled that day. "It was nearly sundown when I saw Smith coming back. I stood bareheaded in my office doorway as he approached ("Two City Marshals," p. 529)." Henry invited Smith to sit, motioning with a sweep of his hand toward a wooden chair.

Henry stared for a moment as if expecting Smith to say something. When the Irishman made no offer to speak, Henry decided to get right down to business. That seemed to be the way this no-nonsense lawman operated. Get down to business.

Henry had already learned some things about Smith. He was from New York City and had been on the police force there. Smith was Catholic, Henry learned. He never swore or drank. He was an intelligent sort. Again and again, Henry asked himself, "How can this gentle man go up against these Texas louts?"

These uncivilized cowpokes and the saloon keepers, gamblers, and brothel keepers that they attracted ruled the town. They got away with whatever they wanted. Henry was afraid that it had been that way for too long. How would this problem ever be solved? Could they ever be tamed by anyone who was not just as reckless and careless as they were? Another desperado?

The problem was that futures and good incomes were at stake in this community. If Abilene could somehow overcome this name, this scourge that hung over it like ominous clouds, then it could very well grow into one of the great cities of the Great Plains. Henry knew that. And many of the businessmen whose stores stood woven among the saloons along the rowdy streets knew it as well.

Mayor Henry also knew that what was settled just now might very well have a great and significant bearing on the future of this town. If the town had any future at all.

Henry remembered that Smith, on his return, "declined to come in, and remained outside, but removed his hat ("Two City Marshals," p. 529)."

The sun shone brightly on Tom Smith that day in Abilene. Soft gusts of wind whipped up dust in the rippling heat, then flipped the cottonwood leaves back and forth. He could have discarded his black suit coat, but that was not his style. The coat covered his shoulder holsters and pistols. He had no intention of flaunting them. He settled matters in another way. He didn't use guns ("Two City Marshals," p. 527-532).[3]

A polite man, Smith's traits of friendliness, calmness in the face of adversity, and understanding of people impressed people he met. But could he tame this town gone bad? That was the only question that Tom Smith needed to answer.

Boom Town

The Abilene that Bear River Tom Smith surveyed in 1870 was a boom town. Cattle were also being shipped from Solomon, Salina, Brookville, and Ellsworth, but Abilene was the leading shipper (Streeter, *The Kaw*, p. 184).

Joseph McCoy had directed so many Texans to The First National Bank of Kansas City that that bank opened a branch in Abilene that summer to cash in on the boom. "Over $900,000 passed over the counter in its first two months of operation there (Dykstra, p. 83)."

For the farmers and cowboys, several stores had located in Abilene. J.B. Northcraft operated a drug store on the corner of First and Cedar. Hodge's general hardware store was open for business. Just south of the tracks on the west side of Cedar, there was the Kuney Southwick Lumber Yard. On Texas Street that summer of 1870, Thomas C. McInerney's boot factory hired twenty bootmakers to keep up with sales to the cowboys. High-heeled, red-topped boots with a Lone Star design sold like hot baths to the Texans.

A favorite store with cowboys and other visitors alike was the Frontier Store operated by Ohioan William S. "Doc" Moon. Doc Moon was an enterprising sort. He saw to it that his store also was the post office. Just inside the front door and over to the left, there was a counter surrounded with a wire cage. It was there that cowboys up from Texas sometimes got word from home. In turn, the cowboys could send cards home to Texas, assuring their loved ones that they had survived the trip, the trail drive up the Chis-

holm Trail. Besides having a post office, Doc Moon's sold grocer-
ies, saddles, rifles, and molasses. A cowboy could buy anything at
Doc Moon's.

Stuart Henry, who lived in Abilene, had sympathy for these
Texas men and boys. Henry wrote of the cowboy, "His home, the
saddle. His personal equipment meant distinctively, his quirt, his
lasso and other equine trappings. His bed-chamber spread out under the broad sky. No tent had he to bother about. His food con-
sisted largely of corn bread (or pones) and 'sow belly' (mast-fed
bacon), liquefied by heady coffee lacking sugar and milk. No fresh
beef, no vegetables; his stove, a hole in the ground, if no 'chuck'
wagon was along. His meals were cooked in a camp skillet and 'et'
mainly with a pocketknife which took the place, one may say, of
table knives, forks, spoons, plates. The water often so muddy it had
to be 'chewed!' (Henry, S., p. 68-69)"

Faced with those hardships during the long, grueling cattle
drive, many a cowboy rode the last few miles into Abilene with
nothing but thoughts of Doc Moon's Frontier Store dancing in his
head. And not all the cowboys came to Abilene to get in trouble.
McCoy wrote, "There are many creditable exceptions,—young
men who respect themselves and save their money, and are worthy
young gentlemen,—but it is idle to deny the fact that the wild,
reckless conduct of the cow-boys while drunk, in connection with
that of the worthless northern renegades, have brought the per-
sonnel of the Texan cattle trade into great disrepute, and filled
many graves with victims, bad men and good men (McCoy, p.
141)."

As it too often happens, the actions of a few often condemn
the entire group. And so it was with the cowboys coming up from
Texas.

Of the saloons and gambling houses, the Alamo, with a forty-
foot front, was the most popular—and the most extravagant. In
season, four bartenders kept busy drawing beer and pouring drinks
for the hot, thirsty cowboys at the Alamo. The fancy bar was the
focal point inside. It was ornate and of polished, brass-trimmed

mahogany. There was a brass rail and shiny knee-high spittoons. Thirsty men lined the bar. Kerosene lamps hung from the ceiling, bringing a yellow glow—and flying insects, in season—to the 120-foot long barroom.

Three sets of double-glass doors extended across the front and greeted the eager cowboy as he stepped inside the fancy saloon. Paintings graced the walls, "in remote but lascivious imitation of Titian, Tintoretto or Veronese." In the words of Stuart Henry, the framed wonders "exhibiting nude women relaxed in beauty prostrate" seduced the men who enjoyed the Alamo's sporting life (Henry, S., p. 267). The young cowboys' first looks were nervous glances. Not until after a beer or two did they risk looking longingly at the nude pictures.

Dazzling mirrors caught the light and reflected it. Many a cowboy was impressed by the colorful bottles of whiskey, rum, and brandy on the back counter. In season, decorated vases of flowers sat around the large room. Music mixed with all this as a piano and violin often created a little culture for these Texas cowboys. Sometimes an orchestra played at the Alamo (Cushman, p. 244).

Across from the polished, brass-trimmed bar were the green cloth-covered gambling tables. Ivory checks were piled on the green cloth. Sometimes cowboys won; most of the time they lost. But most were satisfied with the risk—and the fun.

The sounds, sights, and smells of the Alamo were even exciting: clinking glasses, jingling spurs, men winning and losing. Even the smell of stale beer stayed with many a cowboy after he'd ridden toward camp. Why, after a hard trail ride, dust boiling, cattle stinking, the Alamo just nearly took away a young cowboy's breath.

One such youngster was named J.L. McCaleb. He told of his first visit to Abilene in "My First Five-Dollar Bill." At a saloon (or was it a dance hall?), he and a friend ordered a drink and suddenly, a girl came up to him and placed her hand under his chin. She looked him in the eye, smiled, and said, "Oh, you pretty Texas boy, give me a drink."

McCaleb nervously dug a five dollar bill from his pants and told her "that she could make herself easy; that I was going to break the monte game, buy out the saloon, and keep her to run it for me when I went back to Texas for my other herd of cattle."

McCaleb took his drink and stepped to the monte table, his spurs jingling, leaving the girl standing at the bar. He remembered, "Well, I went to the dealer, put my five on the first card, and won. I now had ten dollars, so I put the two bills on the tray and won. Had now twenty dollars and went to get a drink—another toddy but my girl was gone. I went back and soon lost all I had won and my original five and I went out, found my partner and left for camp (McCaleb, p. 486-487)."

Some cowboys at the Alamo had no desire to return to camp. Instead, they yearned for female companionship of the purchased kind. The Alamo, always considerate of its customers, built a boardwalk out the back door that led to one of the houses of ill repute. Everything a lonesome cowboy could ask for.

What happened to young Mr. McCaleb was not unlike the events played out on many a young cowboy up from Texas for the first, or second, or third time. They were always going to win big at the gaming tables and with the soiled doves. Always, that is, until they got to town and tried their luck.

These cowboys were a hard lot. A Kansas traveler of the period described a cowboy: "In appearance a species of centaur, half horse, half man, with immense rattling spurs, tanned skin, and dare-devil, almost ferocious faces (Brown & Schmitt, p. 64)."

A New York *Tribune* corespondent observed some Texas veterans of the Civil War, now punching cattle, "Some of them have not yet worn out all of their distinctive gray clothing—keen looking men, full of reserved force, shaggy with hair, undoubtedly terrible in a fight, yet peaceably great at cattle-driving and not demonstrative to their style of wearing six-shooters (Brown & Schmitt, p. 64)."

For some cowboys, when they first arrived the beer wasn't cold enough, the saloon wasn't fancy enough, nor were the girls pretty enough. For some, however, after a few hours in a place like the Alamo, all the saloons and all the girls in Abilene looked darned good. And the beer tasted much better. Drunken cowboys wandered the streets, whooping and hollering, drinking their way from one place to the other. And townspeople wondered, would Abilene ever be civilized enough to raise a family?

Joseph McCoy, the founder of the cow town, witnessed cowboys on what he called the "warpath." He was amazed at their uncanny ability to put themselves and the good citizens of Abilene in harm's way and somehow survive it. Concerned about their health, he wrote that they imbibed poison whiskey. McCoy added, "Then mounting his pony he is ready to shoot anybody or anything; or rather than not shoot at all, would fire up into the air, all the while yelling as only a semi-civilized being can. At such times it is not safe to be on the streets, or for that matter within a house, for the drunk cow-boy would as soon shoot into a house as at anything else (McCoy, p. 134)."

It was more than most sober citizens of Abilene would tolerate. Somehow, there had to be an end to this sooner or later. In the meantime, it was necessary to continue to carry on in a civilized and Christian way.

But then, when the sun rose up out of the stockyards, Abilene was a different place. Most of the cowboys were over at the stockyards or outside of Abilene working their waiting herds. The stock growers and the buyers from back East enjoyed a big breakfast, then came together and began working out deals. They leaned on fences at the stockyards, their heads together, swapping stories and mixing business talk in the whole dealing package. Many of the deals for cattle were cut on the big shady porch of the Drover's Cottage.

Despite all these distractions, the people of Abilene saw to it that their first schoolhouse was constructed during 1869. They'd have their civilization in bits and pieces. The school was first. Mathias Nicolay built it of stone "quarried from the river cliffs" at a cost of $2,500; a handsome sum for that day. It was a square structure and was located about a block south of Texas Street near the southwest corner of the town (Henry, S., p. 39).

The Reverend W.M. Downer, a Baptist missionary, and seven local Baptists were instrumental in getting Abilene's second sure sign of civilization, Abilene's Baptist Church. Painted a dull lead color, Stuart Henry's memories of church services there were not kind. Every Sunday morning after a thorough scrubbing and being all primped up, Henry was led to church services. According to young Henry, the clergymen "insisted on violent doses of hell fire, everlasting punishment, infant damnation, with supreme confidence before a small Sunday congregation beset with nightmares and privations during week days (Henry, S., p. 78)." No doubt, the Rev. Downer was just trying to rise to the enormous chore he had of saving Abilene from what he no doubt considered an overdose of sin. Although, as it usually happens, he was administering the cleansing not to those who needed it. The Baptist Church was in operation and issuing "doses of hell fire" by 1870.

And now, in the spring of 1870, Abilene, Mayor Henry, and Bear River Tom Smith were preparing to do something about restoring safety and civilization to this cow town. Smith was confident he could tame the cowboys. Henry was still not sure of Smith. And Abilene was ready to try anything.

The sun was falling away, dropping into the great expanses of tall grass that stretched all the way to the shining mountains when Tom Smith returned to Mayor Henry's office and stepped down from the gray, Silverheels. Mayor Henry stood in the door. Smith spoke first. He said, matter-of-factly, "I haven't seen anything much different from what I expected."

"You mean you will take the marshal's job?" Henry asked, still amazed at this man.

"I think it can be done," Smith said evenly.

Henry, mute, stared back. Struck at this calm response, Henry's jaw dropped. The two stood staring at each other. Finally, Henry cleared his throat, rubbed his beard, and inquired as to how Smith planned on cleaning up this wild, frontier town.

There was an awkward quiet as Smith and Henry stared at each other. Smith didn't answer.

Mayor Henry again cleared his throat and explained the no-gun ordinance that Abilene had passed, but that no one could enforce. Henry laughed and shook his head, "We might as well try to take away their wives—if they had any—as their six-shooters. We posted the ordinance. They tore it down—shot bullets through it. To try to insist would bring on just the trouble we're trying to keep out of. We don't want to force impossible issues."

Henry began to speak again, but before his words came, Smith quietly said, "Post up the ordinance again ordering every person to disarm on coming to town, and," he added firmly, "staying disarmed while here." Henry remembered in 1904 that Smith acknowledged, "Firearms must be given up; that whisky and pistols were a combination beyond control." Smith added, "As well contend with a frenzied maniac as an armed and drunken cowboy ("Two City Marshals," p. 529)."

Henry almost smiled. He cocked his head, trying to figure what was going on in the mind of this man with the quiet determination. The man would be run into the ground by an army of these rowdy Texans. Was he daft? "You don't think that necessary?"

Smith, his voice even, calmly added, "Nobody can handle this town if the cowboys go armed. When they drink," Smith said, his right hand gesturing, "they think only of shooting. If they have nothing to shoot with, their drinking and gambling won't hurt much."

Henry nodded agreement. He understood that. But that was not the point. The cowboys wouldn't give up the guns. And they riled easy if anyone suggested it. Even more dazzled now by this blue-eyed man with the auburn hair and the big, black mustache, Henry asked, "But how on earth would you—one man—disarm them and the drovers—and the professional 'bad men'? It's a little army. One against an army," Henry added, shaking his head.

"I believe it can be done."

"But it will mean a wholesale fight from the word go. They'll turn loose on us."

Smith said, "It won't exactly be a holiday, I admit, but that's the proposition as I see it."

Henry finally said, "All right. You can have new copies of the ordinance from the printer tonight for posting. You can have anything you want if you're sure you control the trump suit. I'll promise you this—we'll stand shoulder to shoulder. I'm tired of stepping among eggs. Our citizens are tired of being run over—kept afraid—hung up in the air."

Referring to the men that went after the cook that was broken out of the new jail, Mayor Henry added, "They showed they would fight the other day. We're inviting peaceful immigration in here by the carload—women and children. And we meet them with what they call Hell Street.

"Ridiculous! Is this a sane, civilized country or has it got the blind staggers? Our residents and farmers want to know who owns the Plains. The settlers have taken up Government land and made improvements on it. The residents have bought lots and made homes. The Texans have bought nothing, paid nothing, have title to nothing." Henry paused, getting his breath.

"Should they rule the roost and drive us all out?" Henry asked, more to himself than to Smith.

The mayor continued, "And I want to tell you we've a lot of old soldiers in that county. I saw them turning out the other day when we had the fight. And there are the Government troops at Riley and Harker—by Godfrey!—if it comes to that."

"I don't reckon we'll need any of them," Smith said.

"Well, we want a marshal with the proper nerve. We'll go to the limit with him, Smith, I guess there's nothing to do now but swear you in."

"Yes, I see my horse is pestered with flies. I don't want him to get out of temper. I'll have to get a fly net. Nothing to worry about tonight, Mr. Mayor. I'll look over the tough spots. It will probably take ten days to know where we are."

"I'll get the Bible. We are somewhat ceremonious. Official custom."

Henry's swearing Bible was near the door. It had been used several times, but showed no unusual wear. The several men that had been sworn to uphold the laws of Abilene hadn't hurt it any. Nor had they done Abilene much good.

There was a small platform on the ground made of pine and nails in front of the door of Henry's office. Smith stood there, his hat off, his gray's reins in his hand.

Smith squinted, facing into the sun. He raised his right hand and placed his left on the Bible. The afternoon sun was low in the sky nearly staring him directly in the eye. Henry, his back to the sun, quickly repeated the solemn words, then added, "This is a grave moment for me as well as you. I'm giving the town over to you. But I'm betting on you—that's all."

Remembering this solemn moment over thirty years later, Henry said, "The bright gleams of the setting sun athwart Smith's square right shoulder, struck me in the face. As he raised his hand for the oath in response to my own, the blinding glimmer of the rays made me lift my other to shield my eyes as I peered searchingly into his own. If I could but picture vividly as the kinetograph the full perspective spread before my vision then, what a priceless treasure for your archives it would be ("Two City Marshals," p. 529)!"

Henry laid the Bible aside and produced a silver badge. He pinned it on Smith. The two men shook hands and Smith turned to his horse, grabbed a handful of mane, swung into the saddle and told Henry, "I'll get the ordinance at the printers tonight, Mr. Mayor. It will be posted over town by morning. I'll report to you at nine."

Smith wheeled the horse, headed toward Texas Street. "Silently," Mayor Henry recalled, "he moved off, and I watched him with misgivings disappear downtown, a third of a mile away ("Two City Marshals," p. 530)."

Mayor Henry watched Smith for a few seconds, then murmured to himself, "That will be nerve!"

Mayor T.C. Henry said later that he felt a measure of guilt as he left his office and walked to his home that evening. He admitted that, despite the good feelings he had about Smith, he did not figure on the new marshal living through the next 48 hours (Henry, S., p. 137).

As to salary, Smith and the trustees settled on $150 a month. They also asked for the resignations of the "old police." Smith was hired for one month only. He was also given permission to hire "a man to assist him." His choice was a man named Robbins, the temporary policeman the night the jail house was raided. [At some time later in the summer, J.H. McDonald, a Canadian was added to the force.] (Cushman, p. 250)

In addition, any arrest and conviction that Smith made meant another $2. And he would earn every penny of it. Abilene was a town that needed taming. Bear River Tom Smith was the man for the job (Records of the City of Abilene, 1871, p. 29, 34).

Disarming

bilene Chief of Police Tom Smith had a plan. Back on Texas Street just minutes after leaving Henry's Railroad Street office, he stepped down from Silverheels and walked briskly from business to business, the board sidewalks thudding under his hurried steps. At each place of business, he explained his plan. His message was simple enough. He could maintain law and order in Abilene, but only if there was some sort of gun control. Would each of the proprietors cooperate in helping him collect the shooting irons of their customers?

Lock up the guns, Smith reasoned. Lock them in racks. Lock the guns in safes or desks. Anywhere, lock them anywhere, but control them. Keep them out of the hands of cowboys and gamblers and the shootings will stop, he explained. Abilene would be peaceful, he reckoned, if they'd just help him control the guns. He'd post a sign in each of their businesses. He'd help them regulate the guns. Besides, he told them, it was good for business.

Over the next days, Chief Smith saw to it that the signs were placed where all could see. In particular, he placed signs in all the businesses:

ALL FIREARMS ARE EXPECTED TO BE DEPOSITED WITH THE PROPRIETOR. (Henry, S., p. 68-69)

Each hotel, store, saloon and bawdy house received a visit from the quiet lawman. Calmly and politely, he explained the reasoning behind checking the guns and how a peaceful Abilene would be more profitable for the proprietors and the cowboys as well. The bad element, the gun-toting cowboys and gamblers down on Texas Street, Smith warned, kept many law-abiding Easterners, their pockets full of money, away from the town. These visitors from the East didn't take kindly to the reputation that Kansas already had, long before Texas cowboys arrived.

Already, since the mid-1850s, Kansas folks had a reputation for not paying much attention to the law. Some historians have argued that the Civil War had actually started in the mid-1850s in "Bleeding Kansas." This war along the Kansas-Missouri border attracted the attention of the slave and non-slave factions east of the Mississippi River. Kansas was a dangerous, lawless place.

With the Civil War over and Kansas more settled, the profits from the rush of cowboys and their herds in off the plains for a few weeks or months each year were good for business. But could a town exist for long with those kinds of activities, those kind of customers? They weren't the kind of men that tamed a country, turned the soil, built communities, and created and nurtured civilization. It would be the stable, hard-working, law-abiding farmer that made Abilene prosper. It would not be the gun-toting, hard-drinking, hell-raising young cowboy that spurred Abilene out of the frontier 19th Century into the prosperity of the 20th Century.

At the same time, if Abilene was to survive and gain economic advantage through this hard time, then the guns must be removed from the reckless men that packed them. If they would leave their weapons with the proprietors, then they might trade with that same proprietor. It was a capital idea. The cowboy would trade where he left his gun. He'd trust the proprietor to look after him and his gun.

One Abilene citizen remembered later, "These proprietors, one after another, agreed to keep charge of the firearms of their customers and even invite such action. They saw in it an advantage in holding trade. Texans would deal where their weapons could be claimed (Henry, S., p.142)."

Understand, there was some bitterness and resistance to Smith's method. But before long, some of the drovers saw the value in keeping their cowboys out of trouble. Cowboys and drovers alike began checking their weapons at a favorite place on riding into Abilene. That built a powerful trust between the cowboy and the owner of the establishment. Cowboys soon saw the value of the ordinance and deposited their pistols with little protest. It was a deal that eventually sat well with the cowboys.

Smith had won, but not without demonstrating that he was fair and evenhanded with everyone he dealt with. He didn't seem to have a mean streak in him. He never attempted to show up a drunken cowboy, nor did he believe in using his guns to get the drop on some trouble maker. There was no point in embarrassing the cowboy, trying to make a fool of him. Smith was up front with those he met and didn't try to strip their pride from them. A cowboy got exactly what he saw in Smith—and just a bit more.

This quiet, calm, no-nonsense approach to law enforcement soon attracted attention. When Chief Smith first encountered cowboys tearing down his signs that ordered guns checked, he would calmly step down from Silverheels and punch the cowboy who had torn down the sign in the face. While the cowboy was reeling from Smith's hard fist, thrashing around in the dust, the marshal would replace the gun order, using tacks and the butt of one of the big pistols he carried in his shoulder holsters. It didn't take long for the cowboys to spread the word. This lawman meant business, but he didn't mean to kill you. This marshal had a different set of rules. It was up to the cowboys to learn how the game was played. Few men cared to go up against this two-fisted, serious law officer. And besides, he was a hard man to dislike. Never boisterous, always quiet, he was out to enforce the law, not humiliate any man.

Abilene was booming, all right. Not only busy with the hustle and bustle of the cattle trade, farmers flocked to the town for the seed and supplies that they needed to plant grain and raise their own cattle. It was Tom Smith's duty to protect them, too. Besides, they were permanent residents. This was their home and they had families. They were living here year around.

But Abilene had not been a boom town for long. The town had come a long way since Joseph G. McCoy stepped off the train in 1867 and saw it for the first time. It took a powerful imagination to visualize a future for the wind-swept grasslands. But Joseph McCoy seldom lacked vision. He wrote later, "Abilene in 1867 was a very small, dead place, consisting of about one dozen log huts, low, small, rude affairs, four-fifths of which were covered with dirt for roofing; indeed, but one shingle roof could be seen in the whole city. The business of the burg was conducted in two small rooms, mere log huts, and of course the inevitable saloon also in a log hut, was to be found (McCoy, p. 44)." And out of that McCoy saw great herds of cattle, hotels, schools, churches, and people.

Whether the mild-mannered Bear River Tom Smith, Abilene's first full-time law enforcement officer, saw such a future for this plains community is not known. If he knew anything, it was to do his job as Abilene's first full-time law enforcement officer. Even though he was only 5'11" and weighed 170 pounds, he was a thinking man. Under that hat he wore was not only a head of thick auburn hair, but also a brain. He had a brain that had been taught to think ahead, to anticipate trouble.

Perhaps in the police training in New York City, Chief Smith had learned how to enforce the law. He knew how to deal with the characters that he might run up against. One of the things he'd learned was the value of enforcing the law from horseback. Soon everyone recognized Smith and his big gray horse making the rounds on Texas Street. The gray and its rider could be seen riding slowly east and west along Texas Street, always right in the middle of the street, always at a calm—almost silent—pace.

But the quiet that came to Abilene with Smith had its interruptions. After just a few days of setting the rules in the rowdy part of Abilene, the handsome chief of police was called out by a character known only to history as "Big Hank." (Some sources say his last name was Hawkins.)

Dressed in typical cowboy fashion, Big Hank was ready for a Saturday night on the town. He wore a large hat and bandanna and a belted revolver resting high on his hip. This tough customer and a few of his followers stepped into the dusty Abilene street on a June Saturday afternoon and challenged the officer on the gray horse.

Winking at his comrades, Hank said, "Are you this rooster of a new marshal who proposed to run Abilene from now on?"

Smith sized up the situation, stepped down from Silverheels and moved in close to Big Hank, close enough that he could smell his foul breath. Speaking so softly that most of those backing up Big Hank couldn't hear, Smith said, "Look, Mister, I am employed as marshal and I shall try to maintain order and enforce the law."

The quiet officer looked by Big Hank, then returned his eyes to him, "Be sensible about this and don't make any trouble."

Hank hitched up his pants and asked, "What do you intend to do about this gun ordinance?" He looked back, winking at those standing just behind him.

Smith's face hardened now. His fists were clenched. The words came, snapping out of his mouth, "See that it is obeyed."

He paused, then quickly added, "I must trouble you to hand me your gun."

Big Hank bristled at that and responded, "The hell you say. No redheaded son-of-a-bitch wearin' a tin badge is goin' to take my gun."

"Your gun," Smith repeated, firmly.

Hank spit an oath and made a move toward his big revolver. Before he could reach it, Smith's right hand was buried in the pit of his stomach and just as quickly, Smith's left hand came up, striking the boisterous cowboy in the chin, snapping his head back and laying him out flat in the Kansas dust.

The astonished cowboys with Big Hank stood shocked, staring at their vulgar friend. One laughed nervously. Slowly, the others backed off, some chuckling, others still too awe-struck at the smashing style used by the new police chief to lay away their loud-mouthed friend.

Tom Smith kneeled, opened the military holster, and took Hank's gun. He nodded to the others and they immediately gave up their pistols. Smith took a strip of rawhide from his belt and laced the guns together by the trigger guards.

Big Hank was starting to stir now. His friends stopped chuckling and stared down nervously at the hulk of a man, not knowing what to say at this unusual posture that he had taken. Finally, when Hank regained his senses sufficiently to understand Smith's words, Smith told him, his voice firm, "Get out of town! Now!"

Mayor Henry recalled, "The news of the encounter was heralded over a radius of many miles. The unique punishment employed was wholly new to cowboy warfare, and every phase of it was debated (Henry, S., p. 62)."

And it didn't take long for another test of Tom Smith's courage. The second test came the very next day, a Sunday. A tough known only as "Wyoming Frank" was the antagonist this time. From a camp on a branch of Chapman Creek northeast of Abilene, Frank bet his cowboy friends that he could go to town and take care of this new police officer.

Frank arrived in town on Sunday morning and went from saloon to saloon on Texas Street, drinking and bragging about how he'd not have his gun taken by some tin-starred officer. After a while, he began boasting that Chief of Police Smith must have heard that he was coming to town and disappeared, afraid to face a man as mean and tough as Wyoming Frank.

It being a Sunday, Smith came riding slowly down Texas Street in late morning, later than his normal time for making the rounds. Wyoming Frank, some braver now with the liquor in his belly, was not hard to find. The cowboy was boasting noisily now about how he was wearing his guns and he planned on continuing to wear his guns. Dared anybody to try to take his guns away. Talked about all the unkindly things he'd do to anyone that dared mention taking his guns.

Smith stepped down off Silverheels and calmly flipped the reins over the hitching rail near the Pearl Saloon. Wyoming Frank was keeping a sharp eye on Smith.

Smith did the same, noting that the big man wore two pistols. During this time, the tall, tough-looking man backed slowly and carefully through the door into the Pearl. (Some claim it was the Lone Star where the action took place.)

A crowd of cowboys waited inside, anxious to see how this new policeman operated. Several were backed up against a crude bar, their big hands holding mugs of warm beer. Wyoming Frank, first mumbling several oaths, then letting fly with a vulgar string of epithets in a loud voice, now stopped in the center of the saloon.

Smith was closing on him. Some remembered seeing a sort of gleam in Smith's eye. But in a flash, he was on Wyoming Frank, slashing at him with his big fists and hammering him to the floor. Some claimed he only hit Frank twice, a double-blow they called it.

Smith quickly relieved the big cowboy of his pistols. As he started to get up, Wyoming Frank cursed at him again. Smith, his expression never changing, slapped the vulgar cowboy across the head with one of his own pistols, knocking him back down on the floor.

Wyoming Frank was more civil when the pain of the six-shooter began to subside. Smith stood over him and ordered, "I give you five minutes to get out of this town and don't you ever again let me set eyes on you."

"For an instant," Mayor Henry related, "all stood dazed and speechless, whereupon the saloon proprietor stepped from behind the bar and said to Smith: 'That was the nerviest act I ever saw. You did your duty, and that coward got what he deserved. Here is my gun. I reckon I'll not need it so long as you are marshal of this town.' Others stepped forward to offer their guns and Smith said quietly, 'Hand your guns to the bartender to keep until you want to go out to camp' ("Two City Marshals," p. 530-531)."

Smith then jerked Wyoming Frank to his feet and headed him, staggering, out the door and into Texas Street ("Two City Marshals," p. 529).[4] On Monday morning after this adventuresome weekend, Smith showed up at the office of Mayor T.C. Henry. Henry had heard of Smith's exploits and was elated. He told the new chief, "Anyone can bring in a dead man but to my way of thinking a good officer is one who brings them in alive (Jameson, p. 54)."

Mayor Henry didn't mention it, but was happy to see his law enforcement officer coming back alive, too. He'd been wrong about Smith not lasting 48 hours and he was glad of it.

Smith always seemed to have the rare quality of being prepared, always ready to do what was necessary. On one occasion, he was down on Texas Street and in a saloon when he heard a ruckus from the street. A Mexican cowboy had obviously had too much to drink and was riding up and down the street yelling at the top of his lungs, "Ca-rach-o! Ca-rach-o!"

Smith let him make a pass or two, then stepped out of the saloon and off the porch into the street. When the Mexican's horse came loping by again, Smith jumped into the path of the horse and rider, grabbed the cowboy's leg and the saddle horn and jerked both man and horse to the ground. Most that saw it attributed it to Smith's athletic prowess and obvious strength. No one remembered if it was a small horse the visitor from south of the border rode.

Smith's ability with his fists baffled most that he came in contact with. The Civil War had left the frontier towns with a gun mentality. That fight had been won with guns, they figured. Millions had fought and learned how to use the weapons. For someone to prefer fists over guns was beyond belief to many that saw and heard of Smith. One Texan noted, shaking his head, "Why, we don't know no more about fist fightin' than a hog knows about a sidesaddle."

Full-time Law Enforcement

In the last three years there have been murdered in Abilene seventeen men, seven of these were ruthlessly murdered through the influence of fancy women and six were slaughtered through intemperance and drunken rows, the remaining four being murdered outright in cool hand-to-hand fights. Murder, lust, highway robbery and prostitutes run the town day and night. Decent women dare not walk the streets, and men who made the town dare not appear on her sidewalks.

—A.W. Robinson,
Western News
April 11, 1870

It was a terrible place, a den of iniquity, in the view of Mr. Robinson. But wait! Robinson had a motive in describing Abilene with such a downslope slant. He lived in Detroit, a farming community a few miles east of Abilene. Robinson had high hopes that the Dickinson County courthouse and county seat would move to his Detroit. Abilene had been the county seat since the spring 1861 election (Jameson, p. 35). Great financial rewards came to those communities that could get the county seat. It was not uncommon for citizens of one town to raid another town in order to change the location of the county government. Sometimes, the county seat would be hauled away in wagons. At other times, men did what Robinson did. They hired a newspaper and tried to convince the people to move the county seat legally. Most realized this and understood the ploy, but for readers not aware of Mr. Robinson's motives, they might assume that these things were really happening in Abilene.

Granted, Abilene in cattle season was not the greatest place to live, but it certainly did not deserve the radical reputation that Robinson was busy creating during that winter of 1869 and 1870. Nevertheless, newspaper articles like this caused many to perceive Abilene as being a wide open town year round.

A visitor fresh off the train in February could never visualize such conditions. On the other hand, an Easterner arriving between May and October might be easily persuaded that Abilene was indeed "the meanest hole in the state." It was the cowboys and the free-wheeling gamblers, as well as saloon keepers and prostitutes who accompanied them who nurtured this kind of perception. The bad phases of Abilene's reputation were stacked into that season of the year when Texas cattlemen drove Texas cattle to town for shipping.

With the coming of fall, leaves dropping, grass turning brown, frost painting anything it could get at, Abilene was a different place. In the winter, the cowboys and the cattle traders were not there. Abilene's reputation cooled like the weather. The streets were safe again. Little children could venture out of the house. Some of the businesses that attracted the cowboy money shut down until the cattle season resumed.

Parents especially liked Abilene winter. Their children walked to the new schoolhouse without exposure to all the saloons along Texas Street. The trip to Sunday morning church had the same off-season advantages. Abilene's peaceful demeanor carried over into early spring. It was only with the appearance of the Texas herds in later spring that Abilene's behavior began to change.

One of Abilene's pioneer citizens, J. B. Edwards, arrived in the middle of May, 1870, before the great herds of cattle arrived and started the 1870 season. Edwards wrote, "I always thought it was well for me that I arrived ahead of the cowboys, as it gave me a chance to get used to what came after by degrees (Henry, S., p. 145)." Mid-May in Abilene was beautiful. The great herds were not there stirring up clouds of dust. The streets were not alive with the devil-may-care cowboys.

Chief of Police Tom Smith was to face the trouble by degrees, too. Big Hank and Wyoming Frank were just two of his problems. As new cowboys arrived with new herds from Texas, there were always doubters.

Like a gang of school boys, the rowdies in town made sport of just who was going to bring this new lawman down. They also wondered just when this lawman was going to be brought down. After all, this hard-fisted law officer was human, wasn't he?

They admitted that Smith had stood up to some tough characters, but there just had to be someone out there who would make him heel like an old dog. And they always knew where to find Smith, either on horseback riding down the street or at the little office that the Abilene Board of Trustees had built for him adjacent to the mayor's office on Railroad Street.

The remainder of the summer of 1870 went easily for Smith. Henry said later, "No guns thereafter were openly worn on the streets of Abilene, nor was Smith ever again publicly affronted. Of course, there were drunkenness and quarreling; dens of iniquity flourished and some murders even occurred; but his tact, courage and good judgment were always adequate to minimize consequences, and without resistance. Smith was alike popular with merchants, gamblers, citizens, and saloon-keepers. In a short time he ruled practically without oversight ("Two City Marshals," p. 531)."

Naturally, the law-abiding, God-fearing citizenry of Abilene appreciated the no-nonsense, law-and-order attitude of their police chief. Merchants felt safer in their places of business. Mothers worried less about their children being accidentally shot or ridden down in the streets. Hotel owners were relieved, knowing that there was someone in town who could handle any problem that arose.

On August 9, the town trustees decided to reward Smith. They raised his salary to $225 a month (Records of the city of Abilene, 1870, p. 37). They made the salary retroactive to July 4, when his first month had been up. He continued to receive the $2 for each arrest and conviction. One source, the (Clyde, Kansas) *Republican Valley Empire* of August 2, 1870, identifies Smith as a deputy and undersheriff of Dickinson County.

On the other side of the tracks, over on Texas Street, there were also folks there who were pleased with the direction the town was taking. Saloon keepers, always plagued with drunken cowboys getting out of hand, need not worry about breaking heads themselves whenever someone got out of hand. The law would do it for them. The risk for gamblers was even relieved since some hard loser was not as likely to pull a gun on them. Smith was popular with everyone. More important, they grew to like the law officer.

From time to time, a cowboy new to the area came to town and had to be introduced to Tom Smith's rules. And sometimes, the balance of power in the community shifted around.

There was a section of Abilene called at various times, The Devil's Addition, The Valley, Texas Town, The Colony, Fisher's Addition, or The Beer Garden. It didn't stay in one place for long, shifting from one section of town to another. It was north of the tracks for a while, then on the southeast corner of town. During those early years, it moved frequently. This was, of course, the popular area of town where the prostitutes, licensed and unlicensed, lived and worked.

There were mixed feelings about these women and their plight. Stuart Henry felt they should be centered in one section of town. That was better, he figured. He recalled, "Fenced off there, the occupants should be forced to stay inside unless on respectable errands like shopping. The plan would remove them from the town itself, including Texas Street, and breed less inclination to dissipation and rioting there (Henry, S., p. 278)."

Otherwise, about four o'clock in the afternoon, the prostitutes began parading along Texas Street, usually in groups of two to six. Most, despite the summer heat, were dressed in long dresses, hats, and long sleeves. In the style of the time, their shape was shown off by the corsets they wore. Kansas wind, being notorious, caused some women to wear lead weights and trace-chains in the hems of their skirts.

All in all, these women generally made themselves up as well as money would allow. They purchased beauty in a bottle from the general store, but home methods were common, too. For example, a popular method of shampooing their hair was to stir up a shampoo concoction of castor oil "and pure whiskey scented with lavender."

Hair styles were varied, but many utilized a curler, "a slate pencil heated over a kerosene lamp chimney." And vanity—and perhaps good business—influenced some. One person noted, "The older prostitutes sometimes colored the gray in their hair with sage tea (Brown, *The Gentle Tamers*, p. 143)."

For cosmetics, cornstarch served as facial powder, honey was used to soften hands and beet juice served as rouge. There was seldom a problem distinguishing between the "painted cats" and respectable town ladies. Town ladies dared not wear make-up for fear they'd be mistaken for "working girls." The presence of these working girls made life uncomfortable for the respectable ladies of Abilene.

Still, the men of Abilene observed these fallen ladies. Young Stuart Henry recalled, "When on parade those temptresses looked gorgeous as Brazilian butterflies, showing themselves, equally with their paramours, flaming and intimidating as well as gallant, their expansive and expensive skirts snapping in the prevailing breezes."

Henry continued, "Hats exploded in daredevil sunbursts of direction." Henry also noted that these working ladies often wore boots. One of the boots held the prostitutes purse; the other boot usually had in it a pistol or a knife (Henry, S., p. 118-120).

Some estimate that a hundred or so prostitutes lived in Abilene during these cow town years. Most lived together, crowded into houses that would barely hold them. Henry recollected, "A few of these Abilene women had killed a man. They did not always hesitate to rob their guests, often enough intoxicated. Thus their brawls were sometimes accompanied by shooting or cutting escapades which altogether made acute disorders in that precinct. Even if a woman had been ordered out of town, she would only have been succeeded by another, perhaps worse (Henry, S., p. 118-120)."

Horse-drawn hacks carried customers to the prostitutes night and day. "Money and whiskey," according to Abilene lumber dealer, Theophilus Little, "flowed like water down hill, and youth and beauty were wrecked and damned in that Valley of Perdition (Brown & Schmitt, p. 66)."

When the cowboys were still wearing pistols, the working girls felt that it was necessary to keep a pistol of their own for protection. As Smith's laws went into affect, the ladies were about the only ones in Abilene with guns. It eventually became necessary for Chief Smith to see to it that the ladies gave up their guns.

Surprisingly, Smith's demands were carried out without difficulty. One historian reported that the ladies got out their guns and "shelled out a wheelbarrow load."

Later, early in September, Smith served notice to the prostitutes living about a mile northwest of Abilene that they would have to clear out. Smith issued the orders one morning and within two days, the working ladies were crowded around the train station buying tickets to Baxter Springs and Wichita. Others left for Kansas City, St. Louis, and Memphis. It was out of season for them in Abilene anyway. And, it was too cold to take a customer down to the Smoky Hill River to go swimming without clothes (Dary, *Cowboy Culture*, p. 218).[5]

Kansas law punished prostitution as a misdemeanor. If the prostitutes did not obey the law, they could be arrested and fined up to $1,000 with county jail sentences of up to six months. Abilene normally fined the prostitutes $5 and the mesdames $10 (Dary, *Cowboy Culture*, p. 218).

The Abilene *Chronicle* was elated: "We are told that there is not a house of ill fame in Abilene or vicinity—a fact, we are informed, which can hardly be said in favor of any other town on the

Kansas Pacific Railway. The respectable citizens of Abilene may well feel proud of the order and quietness now prevailing in the town. Let the dens of infamy be kept out, the laws enforced and violators punished, and no good citizen will ask more."

Chief of Police Tom Smith was commended along with Police Judge Clay C. Kuney. The paper pointed out that they "deserve the thanks of the people for the faithful and prompt manner in which they have discharged their official duties. A grateful community will not forget the services of such efficient officers (Abilene *Chronicle*, Sept. 8, 1870)."[6]

Abilene was calming down a bit. The troublemakers were gone for the winter. Civilized people could relax some now. They could walk the streets without fear of a wild cowboy roaring and whooping down the street, guns blazing. All that was behind them. Abilene was a good place to live—in the late fall and winter.

Why, in mid-October, they even had a fair in Abilene. Dickinson County farmers and their families brought in crafts and canned goods for judging. There were calves and prize hogs. It was a farmer's fair, held southwest of the city on the James Bell farm. Chief Smith was there. Mayor Henry, the principal speaker one day at the fair, spoke optimistically about the future of their town and Dickinson County. But he also talked disparagingly about the cattle trade. He felt it might become a negative element in the growth of Abilene and the surrounding land. He could see a time when cattle would no longer be encouraged in Dickinson County.

Henry then added, "Possibly I am mistaken, but my conviction is, that that time is very near at hand (Dykstra, p. 197)."

Smith had done a fine job and he felt a part of this community now. Whatever the problems at Bear River, Smith was no longer to be held up for that incident. He was no longer Bear River Tom Smith. Abilene was his town, too. As far as he was concerned, it no longer deserved the title of "the meanest hole in the state."

Wild West Lawman

There is very little known for certain about Thomas James Smith's life before Abilene. And that was not uncommon in frontier Kansas. Many of the people in frontier Abilene had no past. Too many times, the land west of the Mississippi River became a haven for someone escaping a past—or a past deed—in the East. A frontiersman might be a step ahead of a mistake made in youth. He might have taken on an obligation, but chose to shirk his responsibility. Or it might be something as common as trying to outwit a banker with an unpaid bill in his fist. Did one of these things chase Tom Smith west? No one knows.

One thing is for certain about Smith: The United States census taker in Abilene for Grant Township, Dickinson County, Kansas, visited Tom Smith and took down vital information. The census lists Thomas James Smith as born in New York. At the time the census taker visited, July 30, 1870, Smith claimed he was 40 years old (Miller & Snell, p. 415).

Mayor Theodore C. Henry talked with Smith about his early life, but still, there was little hard information about Smith or his past. Based on these conversations, the mayor formed some opinions about Smith. Henry wrote of Smith in later years, "He was fairly well educated, reared a Catholic and was clean of speech. I never heard him utter a profane word or employ a vulgar phrase. He neither gambled, drank, nor was in the least dissolute otherwise. I cannot learn that he ever mentioned his family; nor was it ever known that he had any living relatives."

For some reason, Mayor Henry thought that Smith was involved in the Mountain Meadows Massacre in Utah during 1857. Henry claimed this was "nearly authenticated."

The Mountain Meadows Massacre was an incident that occurred in early September, 1857, in the Mountain Meadows Valley of southern Utah. Earlier, Captain Charles Fancher had led a California-bound wagon train through Salt Lake City and southwest toward California. In dealing with the Mormons, there were misunderstandings between Fancher and the Saints. This misunderstanding was exploded by Fancher, voicing his dislike of Mormons and adding some unkind and—as it turned out—unwise remarks about those of that religious persuasion.

Finally, on the night of September 5, 1857, Fancher set the camp for his wagon train about fifty miles west of Cedar City, Utah. At this site, they asked for and received help from a Mormon elder named John D. Lee, his militia, and several Indian allies. The assistance the migrants received wasn't what they'd figured on. The Mormons and the Indians turned on the immigrants and slaughtered all but seventeen children. In later years, Lee was found guilty at a trial and was executed by rifle fire. Was Smith there? Which side was he on? He was too old to have been one of the members of the migrant train. Only little children not old enough to witness against the killers were spared. So what was Smith's role in all of this? Mayor Henry says only that Smith "was a victim in the Mountain Meadows Massacre and left for dead ("Two City Marshals," p. 528)."

There are other possibilities. Several accounts say that Smith quit his job as a New York City policeman and hired on with the Union Pacific Railroad in 1867. These railroad jobs were taken by war veterans from both North and South. In addition, Irish immigrants, failed farmers, and destitute drifters hired on for what was good money at a time when there was an economic slump following the Civil War.

The railroad crews were surveying, grading, and laying wooden ties of cottonwood, cedar, and oak in preparation for the rails. The track layers then came through spiking rails to the ties, headed for the meeting of the tracks of the transcontinental railroad, the union of the Central Pacific and the Union Pacific railroads. The two parts of the transcontinental railroad would eventually meet at Promontory Point, Utah. As the crews of the Union Pacific Railroad laid the ties and rails, always headed west, Smith went with them.

On the Union Pacific, where Smith worked, about every 60 miles there would be an end-of-track railroad town spring up. Some of those towns were located at North Platte, Julesburg, Cheyenne, and Laramie. These railroad workers were making good money and working long, hard hours. (An Irish worker who was semi-skilled earned $35 a month. His room and board was taken care of by the railroad.) These end-of-track railroad towns were a place to let off steam, take the edge off the hard work, and get rid of the money they worked so hard for.

Normally, the end-of-track towns started with a large canvas tent, sometimes with a wooden false front. Other tents sprang up and soon, there was an entire town in the middle of nowhere. Inside the tents was a railroad worker's paradise. There was liquor for sale. Green-clothed gaming tables with real gamblers were there, eager to entertain the worker in a friendly game of cards—until the worker's money ran out. Why, a worker could even have a little romance with women of questionable character—for a fee.

Henry M. Stanley, writing for the *New York Tribune*, visited one of these railroad towns and saw some of the painted ladies. He observed: "These women are expensive articles, and come in for a large share of the money wasted. In broad daylight they may be seen gliding through the sandy streets in Black Crook dresses carrying fancy derringers slung to their waists, with which tools they are dangerously expert. Western chivalry will not allow them to be abused by any man they may have robbed. Mostly everyone seemed bent on debauchery and dissipation (Henry, S., p. 158-160)."

These "hell-on-wheels" railroad towns traced the Union Pacific all the way from Nebraska to Utah. They were hard places.

Each town had its own brawling stories of fights, killings, and thievery. All of them had their problems, but the one at Bear River, or Bear Town, Wyoming Territory, added to the legend of Tom Smith.

This end-of-the-track railroad town was located in Uinta County, east of present Evanston, Wyoming, and for a few months in 1868, 2,000 folks called Bear River home. Then in November, there was trouble. Since September, there had been a persistent rumor that claimed the tiny community was going to be the winter terminus of the Union Pacific Railroad. That meant that instead of a temporary encampment, Bear River might become permanent—until spring. Therefore, this is where the workers would live and spend their money. By mid-November, it was obvious that winter was fast arriving. The laying of track would soon end for the year. Even more, it looked as if Bear River would be the place.

With the rumor came people, described by some as riff-raff and trash, all determined to "mine" the pocketbooks of the hardworking railroad construction crews. The regular prostitutes were there, as were the gamblers. Barmaids, dance hall girls, and the like were lured by easy money and excitement. Swindlers, men and women, arrived, determined to wrest the money away from the hard working railroad people at this winter encampment.

In addition to the main tents, additional canvas tents and false-fronted frontier buildings sprang up that fall. The town and those living there were headed for trouble. Some were dead set against this new evil that had befallen the little community at the end of nowhere. It was a hard land a long way from civilization, but to some of the residents that did not mean that it had to be lawless. A vigilance committee formed as a reaction to the lawlessness problem.

And just what happened? One version of the story is as follows. As it has so often happened down through history, justice was not always been meted out justly. One crisp November night, the vigilantes decided to arrest, judge, sentence, and hang three fellows.

They hanged them near the railroad track as a reminder to others in Bear River and to those arriving in Bear River.

As the three hanged men twisted and turned in the early morning breeze, several of the railroad workers stepped out of their tents into the dawn. Below, along the tracks, they could see the bodies. Who were they? they asked. Were the victims anyone they might know?

Several of the railroad workers walked down to the corpses. The blackened faces looked down, necks distended, and for a while no one was certain who these unfortunate were. But then someone pointed out that they had notes pinned on them. Pieces of paper with crude words scrawled on them were pinned to the dead men's coats: "Warning to road agents."

About then someone recognized one of the corpses. He wasn't a road agent, he was a brother to a man who lived in the railroad camp just outside of Bear River. Someone set off to fetch the deceased's brother.

When the brother arrived, he verified that it was indeed his brother who was hanging so grotesquely from the rope. He was overcome with anger, then grief, but recovered sufficiently to do what was necessary. The men helped the distraught brother retrieve the corpse from the deadly noose. They cut the body down. It was a gruesome sight. The longer they huddled around, looking at the body, seeing the brother's grief, the more rage built in them to set the scales of justice right. With their anger growing, they plotted their revenge on those in town who had made this dreadful mistake.

The railroad men, amidst shouting and cursing, collected their guns and marched toward Bear River. Some say their first stop was a saloon conveniently located in their path. Their plan was to lift there spirits some, collect their thoughts, and plot their next move. There inside the canvas-walled saloon, they did what irate, grieving brothers and friends sometimes do. They drank too much. They neglected their duties. They failed to act swiftly and carry out their version of justice without delay. As a matter of fact, they drank enough and were so tardy in acting that a bunch of men, a hastily put-together vigilante group quickly disarmed and jailed them.

Meanwhile, back at the construction camp, others heard of the hangings. Like the others, they did not take kindly to the fact that three of their own had been hanged. Soon word spread that a group of their fellow laborers had been jailed. Now they were really angry, full of venom and ready to take on the entire town of Bear River. It was November 19, 1868, when the railroad workers, armed with pickaxes, mauls, rifles, and torches as instruments of destruction, marched on Bear River. Whiskey fueled their determination. The crowd gave them courage. Their anger was vented first at the jail.

The rowdy railroad workers stormed the little building, released the prisoners, shot the town marshal and left the jail in flames. Through the rolling smoke, the mad mob continued on, destroying the tent that housed the printer and the press of the Frontier Index. They were set on wiping out this town responsible for killing their fellow railroad workers. A general store was their next target.

The terrified vigilantes had, in the meantime, armed themselves in preparation for the gang of raucous railroad workers. They gathered at the general store and were handed all the guns and ammunition they needed to stand off the mob bearing down on them.

By the time the gang of railroad workers came in sight, the vigilantes had fortified themselves and were ready for anything. From inside the general store, the heavily-armed vigilantes laid down a hail of lead and drove off the rattled railroad workers.

Over the next hours, the siege continued. Still, it was little better than a standoff. Neither side seemed to make any progress. To balance the scales in their favor, the vigilantes sent for the military at Fort Bridger. The next day, United States Army soldiers arrived from the fort and declared martial law, thus restoring peace to Bear River.

In most accounts of the affair at Bear River, Tom Smith is the heroic leader of the gang of railroad workers. In some accounts, Smith stands in the open, feet spread, guns blazing until he is wounded by a townsman's bullet. Some say that when the Union Pacific end-of-track moved on, Smith stayed behind to let his wounds heal. Others, including the *Utah Desert News* of December 24, 1868, claimed that Bear River Tom Smith was sent to the Salt Lake City Penitentiary for his role in leading the Bear River riot.

Following a short term in jail, the story continues, Smith used his reputation as a fearless fighter to take on the job of peace officer in several railroad towns. It was while serving in such a capacity at the Kansas Pacific Railroad base of Kit Carson in eastern Colorado that Smith heard that Abilene was looking for a policeman (Stanley, p. 165-167).

Stranger to Fear

he day broke clear, the sun a glaring bright ball in the eastern sky that October 23, 1870. It rose out of the empty stock pens at the east side of Abilene. Not even the echoes of the bawling, milling cattle could be heard. Pools of water stood here and there inside the weathered fences, the last of the summer's flies settling over them, feeding in hopes of living a little longer. Soon the ground would freeze the hoof prints of cattle long gone to the slaughter houses in the East, leaving only a memory of the lowing stinking cattle from the past summer.

And so, fall settled easy over Abilene. It was good time, a pleasant time in the community. People smiled at each other on Sunday mornings on their way to the only church in town, the Baptist Church. Little children played in the yards of their comfortable homes and even ventured into the dusty streets to ride stick horses and "bang, bang" their wooden guns in the style of the wild cowboys, now returned to Texas.

The weather turned cooler as the prairie winds shifted and began blowing out of the north and northwest. No longer was there a threat of the maddening, twisting winds from the southwest. Winter was just weeks away, but there would be pleasant fall days before the snow clouds rolled out of Canada and into the heart of the Great Plains.

In town, a sort of pall had settled over Abilene's hard streets and hardy people. They'd huddle around a red-walled stove, warding off the frigid winds and complaining about there being nothing between Abilene and Canada to stop it. But the long winter months would renew their hope, hope for a better season next year. Much of their wintertime would be spent keeping warm. They'd not worry about the rowdy Texans this winter. They'd not worry about all the trouble those Texans brought to town.

For Tom Smith, he sometimes felt as if he wasn't earning his money during these quiet times. Certainly, during the summer, his task had been too much for one man. He confronted all kinds of trouble and stood up to it. Never shirked his duty nor ran from trouble. Now, that was behind him.

Smith's deputies, James H. McDonald, the Canadian, and Robbins had been let go. Abilene didn't need the extra men to police the town in the off season. McDonald hired on with Dickinson County Sheriff Joseph A. Cramer's office as a deputy sheriff. [There is evidence that McDonald was acting marshal in Abilene and that Tom Smith served Dickinson County as undersheriff. Some say Smith took the job of deputy U.S. Marshal sometime before November 1870, but historian Harry Sinclair Drago searched Justice Department records and found no evidence that Smith was ever a deputy U.S. Marshal (Drago, p. 81). On the other hand, in July, Smith rode to southeast Nebraska in pursuit of a horse thief named Buckskin Bill. Some of the stolen horses were sold at Pawnee City and Smith had a difficult time getting them back, but he was successful. Buckskin Bill was lodged in jail at Brownville while his accomplice was being held in the Nebraska City jail. Smith went on this mission with the title of Dickinson County undersheriff (*Republican Valley Empire*, Aug. 2, 1870).]

No one is certain what Smith's plans for the future included. None claimed him as a close friend. His conversations seemed to have been mainly with Mayor Henry. His future was unpredictable, but promising. As it turned out, fate settled all the details of Smith's future.

And so it was that on that quiet, fall Sunday, October 23, 1870, Abilene Chief of Police Tom Smith's future was being decided. It was being decided not by him, but by two men living about ten miles northeast of Abilene on Chapman Creek. Two men, a Scotsman and an Irishman, had come a long way, carrying with them their prejudices. Now a world away and halfway across the North American continent, they laid the groundwork for the future of Thomas James Smith.

As happened too often on the frontier of the 19th Century, stories—including eyewitness accounts—get mixed and mangled. Point of view tarnishes truth and ordinarily honest men remember only what they want to remember. Long running relationships among neighbors around Abilene were few, seeing that the area had barely been settled a decade. So who had the story right? Who was at fault? Who stepped outside the law?

In the matter of the Scotsman and the Irishman who were destined to arrange and execute the fate of lawman Tom Smith, it was no different. The stories were numerous with an uncommon number of variations. The question: Where was the truth of the matter?

One story has one of the men, a former buffalo hunter named Andrew McConnell, a big Scotsman born in Massachusetts, saddling up and riding out early that Sunday morning, October 23. He had secured his humble dugout, packed an old cloth sack and, with his big buffalo rifle, rode out over the grassy plains in search of fresh meat, preferably a deer.

After a time, McConnell aimed his horse toward his property and rode back to his dugout. He'd dug a hole out of the side of an embankment, then built the front and one side from grass sod bricks. The door, or the excuse for one, was of wood planks he'd bought. A neighbor remembered McConnell's dugout: "It was built into a hillside, and the door was at the end of a sort of ditch (Stambaugh, in Henry, S., p. 200)."

As McConnell rode nearer his dugout, he realized that he had company. It was a neighbor, John Shea, and Shea was busy herding his cattle across McConnell's land. There was a good grazing spot not far away and the shortest path to it was across McConnell's property. Oh, Shea could get there by going around, but it took time and walked fat off the cattle.

McConnell knew all this. He and Shea had gone over it before. The big Scotsman knew it was shorter across his property. But he'd have none of it, Shea driving his cattle over his land. As a matter of fact, it hadn't been long before this that two yoke of oxen had strayed and wandered into Shea's cornfield. The oxen were hungry and they knocked down some corn and ate some, too. These wayward oxen belonged to McConnell and his neighbor, Moses Miles.

Shea was upset when he found the oxen in his corn. Who would let their oxen run loose like that? With the help of his family, Shea chased the oxen out of the corn and penned up the errant animals. When McConnell and Miles came looking for the strayed oxen, Shea insisted that they pay for the lost corn. He wouldn't let the oxen go otherwise.

The men had words. Why didn't they take care of their oxen? That action did not set well with McConnell and Miles, and they said so. There were bitter words, words that caused men in the West in the late 1800s to consider killing. McConnell admonished Shea not to drive his cattle across McConnell's homestead, a shortcut to the good grass. Warned him against it. Said he'd not stand for it.

Walter D. Nichols, an Abilene resident, picks up the story here. Nichols knew McConnell and Miles. He wrote, "A few days before the fight , I had been to Clay Center hunting horses which had strayed from the Bartell ranch. On my return I stopped at McConnell and Miles' cabin and ate supper with them. They had corn bread and sorghum molasses and it tasted mighty good. I visited with them several hours then on to Bartell's with the horses."

Nichols, too, had heard about the strayed oxen and how Shea'd penned them up. Nichols said it was true. It happened that way. McConnell and Miles were still upset about it. And wouldn't you know, Shea defied McConnell and had his herder drive the cattle across McConnell's land the very next day. It was a foolish thing for Shea to do, but he did it.

McConnell, armed with his buffalo gun, met Shea's herder and turned him away. The men exchanged angry words, but McConnell's fight was with John Shea, so he let the herder go. When the herder returned the cattle to Shea, Shea grew angrier. He'd not put up with this. He blurted, "Tomorrow, I will take them across there myself (Nichols, unp. ms. Dec. 26, 1931)."

The next day, sure enough, Shea came riding along, herding several head of cattle in front of him. McConnell would not stop him this time. They'd sort this out. Come to a settlement of some kind.

McConnell saw Shea coming from a distance. He figured this would happen. But how could Shea do this? McConnell's blood was up. They'd settle this once and for all.

McConnell grabbed up his buffalo gun, checked the load, and stepped out of the dugout to face Shea. Shea was defying him. He was forcing McConnell's hand. This man just didn't understand. He'd warned him. Maybe he'd pay attention to his big rifle. Besides, McConnell reminded himself, he didn't like Irishmen and Shea was an Irishman.

Moses Miles, a Massachusetts Yankee, heard McConnell and Shea shouting at each other. It didn't take long to figure out what was going on. He hurried toward the angry voices.

What happened next was agreed on by both Miles and McConnell. Both men claimed that Shea produced a pistol. He then drew down on McConnell, thumbed the hammer and jerked the trigger. Twice he did this. Twice, nothing happened. Shea snapped the pistol twice, they claimed. The powder did not ignite; the balls did not fire.

Frantic now, Shea was bewildered, looking at the pistol and probably getting an eye full of the big rifle that McConnell was bringing to his shoulder. Shea thumbed the hammer again. Maybe this one would fire. But before Shea could drop the hammer on another chamber, McConnell's big gun bucked and spit flame and black powder smoke. He shot Shea. Shot him through the heart. Left a big hole in his back. Shea, a dumb look on his face, was dead before he tumbled off the horse and hit the Kansas sod.

McConnell, according to the popular story, was remorseful now. He rode to fetch a doctor. No one's certain when this happened or how quickly a doctor was brought into action. When the doctor did arrive, there was nothing he could do short of pronounce Shea dead.

Word quickly spread among the Irish settlers in the area. They heard that the big Scotsman had killed Mr. Shea. Why'd he do it? they wondered. Was it just a Scotsman killing an Irishman? They did not take kindly to the Scotsman killing one of theirs.

McConnell was no fool. He was aware of these differences, but he'd be ready if they did come shooting. He had built his dugout well. Being so far from town and never knowing who might come up on you in the country, it was smart to fortify your dugout. Only the wall with the door and the wall with a window were exposed. He could see from them at the same time. If there was any plan to get the big Scotsman that killed poor Mr. Shea, it did not materialize.

A blast of winter came down from the North on Tuesday, the day that McConnell, and the little Yankee, Moses Miles, appeared for their hearing about the shooting. They shivered some as they stepped onto the front porch of Justice of the Peace Andrew S. Davidson's house a mile or so southeast of Enterprise. With them was their lawyer, G.W. Ferguson. They wanted to be on the safe side in this preliminary hearing.

Davidson, a Union Army veteran from Pennsylvania, had been duly elected Justice of the Peace for Center Township, Dickinson County. He had been in Kansas since the fall of 1866 when he'd homesteaded 80 acres south of Enterprise. (Enterprise is located due south of Detroit and southeast of where McConnell killed Shea.)

Davidson greeted the men as they stepped into the small room that he used as an office, the bright sun splashing light on the floor.

Attorney Ferguson was from nearby Old Detroit. McConnell was somewhat nervous, but told his story. Miles verified it, said that's the way it happened. Sherwood Davidson, sixteen years old then and the son of Andrew S. Davidson and his wife, the former Elizabeth R. Murphy, stood quietly in the corner and listened to the men talk. It was so simple the way young Davidson heard it. He remembered what happened that morning and told it some sixty years later.

"The affair, as nearly as I can remember," Davidson related, "was that Shay [sic] undertook to drive some stock across McConnell's field. McConnell was there at the time and was armed with a rifle. McConnell warned Shay not to drive the cattle that way, and Shay, who was on horseback, pulled a revolver and snapped it twice at McConnell, but before he had time to snap it again, McConnell raised his rifle and shot and killed Shay."

Davidson added, "They had had trouble before, and the day previous Shay's men tried to drive stock across that ground, but were prevented by McConnell. The next day Shay came with the cattle." So there was the story. Just like Miles and McConnell told it.

Since there were no other witnesses to the killing, Justice of the Peace Davidson accepted the testimony and declared that the incident was a simple case of self-defense. Hadn't Shea tried to fire at him? And didn't McConnell deserve the right to defend himself? McConnell was not charged.

To be on the safe side, the senior Davidson suggested that his son, Sherwood, accompany McConnell six or seven miles north to J.M. Shephard's place. Davidson accompanied McConnell, turned him over to Shephard and rode back to his home south of Enterprise (Davidson, unp. ms. Jan. 10, 1932).[7]

There was considerable doubt about just how Shea's killing took place for the neighbors who knew John Shea, his wife and their three children. For them, the story told to Justice of the Peace Davidson was not acceptable. For them, there was something wrong with the story. Over the next days, this uneasiness and doubt spread. There was talk. Perhaps they ought to see to justice themselves. And soon, there was some evidence that McConnell feared for his life. The Irish in the neighborhood were not satisfied that McConnell killed in self-defense. Shea's neighbors claimed that Shea had been murdered.

It became apparent that the Irish and others in the neighborhood would not be satisfied without a warrant being issued. The Abilene *Chronicle* of November 3, 1870 reported: "It afterward appeared to some of the neighbors, from unmistakable circumstances, that Shea was not the aggressor." John Ryan asked for a warrant.

On John Ryan's affidavit, the warrant for the re-arrest of Andrew McConnell was issued by Eliphalet Barber, Justice of the Peace. The affidavit charged that "on or about the 23rd day of October, 1870, John McConnell shot and killed John Shay." It would be up to Dickinson County Sheriff Joseph Cramer to serve the warrant.

But there was a problem. Sheriff Cramer was seriously ill and had been since September. He was in no shape to serve a warrant, nor did anyone expect him to. (He died on December 26, 1870, less than two month later.) Sheriff Cramer assigned James H. McDonald to issue the warrant.

Deputy Sheriff McDonald was uneasy about his task, but set out to do it, the warrant tucked away neatly in an inner coat pocket. The ride northeast to McConnell's place was uneventful. McDonald found the dugout; he found McConnell. Before he could step down off his horse, McConnell shouted a warning. He threatened McDonald and told him not to get down. He wasn't welcome.

That was enough excitement for McDonald. He wouldn't challenge McConnell. He reined his horse away from McConnell's dugout and clucked him back toward Abilene.

Somehow, back in Abilene, McDonald sought out Marshal Smith. Would he serve the warrant? Smith had dealt with tougher men than this, McDonald figured. Smith agreed to serve the warrant.

On November 2, a bleak Wednesday, Undersheriff Tom Smith, accompanied by Deputy Sheriff J.H. McDonald, rode northeast out of Abilene toward McConnell's land. On the way, they stopped at Bill Lamb's and talked to him about McConnell. Smith should be careful, Lamb warned. McConnell feared the Irish, Lamb explained.

"McConnell is a fighter," Lamb told Smith, "and won't be turned loose among those Irish." Smith, an Irishman himself, had to wonder at what he would find. The wind kicked up some now as he and McDonald rode on, drawing nearer and nearer to their destination. Birds darted in and out of the tall grass, slipping along with wind. Winter snow would soon fly and the land would be replenished when it melted with the spring. The sharp wind cut right through their heavy coats. It was a miserable day to be out like this.

The McConnell dugout lay just ahead. A wisp of smoke spiraled from the crude chimney. The blustery wind caught the smoke and made it disappear. At a safe distance from the structure, McDonald reined his horse to a stop. Smith did the same, then stepped down, his saddle creaking.

Smith took a deep breath, said nothing to McDonald, but got right to his business, striding toward the dugout. He heard McConnell yell something, but couldn't tell what. The wind killed the words. But as Smith drew nearer, he heard threats, warnings.

Smith stopped outside the dugout and began talking to McConnell through the window. Where was the warrant? McConnell wanted to know. Read it to me, he insisted. Could Smith promise that the Irish wouldn't kill him on the way to town? Or what about them coming in the jail after him? Could Smith guarantee his safety?

This talk was getting Smith nowhere. He had a warrant to serve. That's all there was to it. Serve the warrant. Do his duty. Arrest the suspect. Take McConnell back to Abilene. As simple as one, two, three. And time was wasting.

Several versions exist of what happened next. One says that the warrant was read through the window and McConnell shot Smith in the chest. Just like that. Shot him without warning. Smith got to his shoulder holster, pulled his pistol and returned the fire, wounding McConnell in the side.

A second version has Smith reading the warrant and then pushing by Moses Miles who was blocking the door. The big Scotsman picked up a rifle. Smith struggled for the gun with McConnell. The buffalo gun roared, striking Smith in the chest. Smith managed to pull one of his revolvers, blasting and wounding McConnell.

Still a third version has Smith growing impatient and shooting through the window, grazing McConnell's side. The shooting then became general with Smith taking a bullet in the right lung.

Where was Deputy McDonald all this time? He had stayed with the horses a short distance from the dugout. One version has McDonald walking toward the dugout just before the shooting began. Miles, armed with a rifle, warned him away. At about that instant, a shot came from inside the dugout and McDonald decided it was time to retreat. This version claims McDonald mounted his horse and rode toward Abilene, his mind more on his own safety than that of Smith's.

Another story has McConnell and Miles in the field working when Smith and McDonald approached. They spotted the lawmen, dropped their tools and ran for the dugout. Smith, in this version, called out that he had a warrant. The shooting commenced with Smith taking a hit in the lung. The gunfire then became general, with McDonald and Miles firing at each other as Smith and McConnell struggled over a rifle. Miles, according to this story, was hit by gunfire from McDonald, but continued firing, eventually running off McDonald.

The last version has Miles firing at McDonald, running him off. McDonald retreated, but not to his own horse. He fled to a nearby claim a half mile or more west, taking a pony from there and riding back to Abilene to report that he figured Smith had been killed.

What really happened? A man named Samuel Haines (Hines) saw the whole thing from a safe distance—and from behind a tree. Smith and McDonald stopped at Haines' claim, about a half mile from McConnell's. Haines rode along with them and reported seeing Miles run off Deputy Sheriff McDonald. It was after that when Smith wrestled McConnell outside the dugout. It was there that Miles came up and began clubbing Smith over the head with a gun. There is no evidence that Miles was hit by gunfire.

Did McDonald run? Was he a coward? J.B. Edwards, an Abilene resident and member of the posse that went after the two killers, said, "Miles kept trying to get his gun to go off, but it persistently refused to do so, and yet McDonald was so much afraid of a gun, even of that kind, that he made no effort in any way to get in where Smith was. No one except McConnell and Tom Smith were in the dugout when a shot was fired inside."

Edwards continued, "As quick as McDonald heard it he took to his heels and fled across the prairies. Leaving his horse where he had tied him, he made for the nearest claim, one-half mile or more west, and, finding a pony, mounted him and came to Abilene as fast as possible, reporting that Smith was killed. In a very few minutes a posse (including myself) was off for the scene of the conflict (Stanley, p. 203-204)."

Charles F. Gross added to the McDonald role in all of this. Gross was at the Drover's Cottage in Abilene the afternoon of the killing of Smith. Gross minced no words. He pointed out, "Smith was deserted by McDonald."

Gross recalled, "I can see him (McDonald) now as he rode up to the front door of Drovers' Cottage, dismounted, came into the barroom and leaning against the bar with a drink of whiskey in his hand blubbered out the yarn he told."

Gross continued, "There being no one to dispute him, the story had to go, but I can still recall the looks that passed between men present who, I knew, had been raised from birth to eat six-shooters. It was so rank that no one could say a word.

"I'll never forget it," Gross said (*J. B. Edwards Collections*).

If McDonald was considered a coward, it did not seem to bother the mayor or the people of Abilene since he worked the next summer as an assistant to Wild Bill Hickok, the policeman hired in Abilene during 1871. Another report has McDonald hiring on as marshal of Newton, Kansas, at some later date.

As to what occurred next up on Chapman Creek at the McConnell dugout on that fate-filled Wednesday, there seems to be general agreement. Smith, although lung shot, and McConnell, considerably bigger than Smith, grappled, with Smith holding his own. But then the third player came into the already lurid picture. Little Moses Miles, his face twisted with hate and fear, slipped behind Smith and began clubbing him over the head with a pistol. Smith, who had been spitting up great spurts of blood from the lung shot, now was bleeding freely from the head wounds made by the heavy handle of Miles' pistol. His vision was blurred. His strength was leaving him.

Smith reeled, trying to get away from this bad situation, his rock-hard fists had no snap left to them. His big hands no longer delivered justice. His knees were somehow bent, weak, and refusing to hold him up. The blood taste fouled his mouth. He shook his head trying to regain his senses. This had gone all wrong, he suddenly realized. A sort of dazed bewilderment spread over his handsome, but pale and blood-streaked, face.

So this was the way it happened? This is the way a man was to die.

Haines, still hiding behind the tree, watched as Miles hammered at Smith until he beat him to the ground. Haines saw Miles and McConnell drag the senseless Smith to the woodpile. Miles looked around, then took an ax and slashed at Smith's neck, the blade chopping through bone and flesh, until the handsome head was almost completely chopped off.

The Abilene *Chronicle* had the story the next day. Their version follows: "Upon reaching the dugout they (Smith and McDonald) found McConnell and Miles. Officer Smith informed McConnell of his official character and that he had a warrant for his arrest, whereupon McConnell shot Smith through the right lung; Smith also fired, wounding McConnell; the two being close together grappled; Smith, although mortally wounded, was getting the better of McConnell, when Miles struck him on the head with a gun, felling him senseless to the ground, and seizing an ax chopped Smith's head nearly from his body. At this stage of the tragedy officer McDonald returned to this place for assistance (Abilene *Chronicle*, Nov. 3, 1870)."

McDonald's story fell on a stunned, but angry crowd of citizens in Abilene. Disbelief reigned for a time. There were those who hoped by some miracle Smith was not dead. Surely after a long summer of solving Abilene's legal problems with all kinds of toughs from Texas, this could not happen to this man, nearly invincible in the eyes of many in Abilene. It just couldn't happen. Not to Marshal Smith.

A posse came together quickly. There was cursing and angry shouts, men holding back tears and swallowing sobs. Disbelief was turning to anger. Soon, they tightened the collars on their coats and rode for McConnell's. Hardly a word passed from their lips on the ride. Now and then one or the other shook his head, still stunned at the story that had been brought to them. It couldn't be true.

As they neared the McConnell dugout, there were no signs of life. With guns drawn, they walked their horses closer to the rude hovel. Then someone spotted it. Still, there was disbelief. Smith's lifeless—and nearly headless—body lay near the woodpile. Some of his blood had soaked into the ground. Already it had turned a deep red, almost black. They all took a look, most a quick look. Then more disbelief.

W.S. Stambaugh was one of the first ones to arrive at the dugout after the shooting. He claimed Smith had ridden through Detroit on his way to McConnell's and stopped and asked directions. Stambaugh, a friend of Smith's, warned Smith that he'd eaten dinner at the hotel in Detroit with McConnell just days earlier. McConnell, according to Stambaugh, was not in a good mood.

Smith continued on toward McConnell's. Stambaugh remembered what happened next: "In an hour," Stambaugh recalled, "a young man rode into Detroit, saying that McConnell had murdered him (Smith). I jumped on a horse and rode to the McConnell dugout."

Stambaugh admitted that no one really knew what happened. "Two shots were heard," he said. "McConnell was shot through the hand, Smith in the breast. They grappled and struggled into the open air, Smith with a mortal wound, giving McConnell a fearful battle. Smith got McConnell down and was either getting the handcuffs out of his pocket or attempting to put them on his prisoner when Miles, who was McConnell's partner, came up behind and, taking an ax, buried its blade in Smith's head, striking three blows and almost severing the head from the body (Stambaugh in Henry, S., p. 200)."

Posse member J.B. Edwards arrived a little later. He related in the Abilene *Chronicle* in 1896, "On arriving there we found Smith's body lying some ten yards from the dugout with his head severed from the body excepting the skin on the back of the neck. McConnell and Miles had fled (Henry, S., p. 200)."

Young Sherwood Davidson, who had been in on the hearing that had determined that McConnell had shot Shea in self-defense, had a slightly different story of what happened when Smith went to the dugout. He said that Smith walked to the door of the dugout. There he found Miles sitting with a Spencer carbine in his hands.

McConnell demanded to know what authority that Smith had to arrest him. Davidson said that Smith pulled his pistol and answered, "This is my authority." With that, Smith shot McConnell in the hand, the bullet continuing on and grazing his side. Miles reacted by placing the carbine nearly against Smith and pulling the trigger.

"It is my recollection," Davidson continued, "he laid the rifle down for some reason and picked up a shot gun and went out after McDonald and snapped it at him. McDonald ran away. Then he came back to the dugout and Smith and McConnell had wrestled from inside the dugout clear out to the woodpile and Smith had McConnell down."

It was at this time that McConnell called out to Miles, "He is getting his knife out to kill me."

Miles grabbed the ax and struck Smith twice, the second stroke in the neck, nearly taking his head off.

Davidson said, "There were only two shots fired, the one Smith fired at McConnell and the one Miles fired at Smith, and they both took effect (Davidson, p. 1-2)."

Smith's auburn hair was matted with blood, the head lay hacked from the body except for a flap of skin that attached it to the athletic body. The handsome blue eyes stared eerily out of the once handsome head. It was a hard scene even for men that still remembered the hard scenes of a horrible Civil War.

Some members of the posse were now motivated even more to go after the killers. The horses that Smith and McDonald had ridden to the scene were no longer there. Tracks away from the scene of the killing looked as if the horses had been ridden south. The posse took up the trail, riding south.

Two and one-half miles later, the posse came to the Long place. Mrs. L.H. Long recalled, "McConnell and Miles stopped at our house after the fight and washed the blood off their hands at our pump. McConnell was shot through the hand. They left their horses, saddles, and bridles with Mr. Long and told him to keep them until they called for them but they never came back." (The Longs lived in the southeast corner of the NE 1/4 of Section 28 in Hays Township, Dickinson County.) (Long to Humphrey, unp. Ms. Dec. 26, 1931)

It was nearly dark by now. The cold and excitement of the afternoon had tired many in the posse. Some were hungry and longed for warmth in out of the night air. The trail was growing harder and harder to follow. Soon, the weary, frustrated posse lost the trail of the killers.

In the meantime, back at McConnell's dugout, several men wrapped Smith's body and head in a blanket, tied it up and hauled it back to Abilene. Mayor Henry recalled three decades later in a story in the *St. Louis Globe Democrat*, "An examination afterward proved that the wound from the Winchester would have been fatal, and his desperate fight after receiving it showed plainly the quality of the courage of this remarkable man (Henry, S., p. 201)."

On Thursday morning the Abilene *Chronicle* announced that the funeral would be on Friday. Continuing, the newspaper expressed the grief of the town: "Our citizens had learned to respect Mr. Smith as an officer who never shrank from the performance of his duty. He was a stranger to fear, and yet in the private walks of life a most diffident man. He came to this place last spring, when lawlessness was controlling the town. He was at once employed as chief of police, and soon order and quiet took the place of the wild shouts and pistol shots of ruffians who for two years had kept orderly citizens in dread for their lives. Abilene owes a debt of gratitude to the memory of Thomas James Smith, which can never be paid. Although our people will never again permit the lawlessness which existed prior to his coming to the town, yet it will be a long time before his equal will be found in all the essentials required to make a model police officer (Abilene *Chronicle*, Nov. 3, 1870)."

Injustice Stings

It was Thursday when the residents of Junction City, east of Abilene, got the news of the Smith killing. The *Junction City Union* had part of the story, but varied considerably on several points. Marshal Smith, on arrival at McConnell's dugout said he was looking for McConnell and McConnell answered from where he sat with "a gun between his knees." The Union reported that Smith told McConnell that he was under arrest. Without saying a word, McConnell brought up the gun and fired, striking Smith in the right lung.

The Junction City account claimed that Deputy McDonald was in the fight. The paper said he fired on Miles in an effort to help his fellow lawman Smith. There seems to have been a lull in McDonald's attack, because McConnell and Miles proceeded to beat up on Smith, wrestle him out into the open, knock him down and chop his head off. Then, according to the *Union*, they got time to deal with McDonald. They turned their wrath on him. According to this report, Deputy McDonald bravely laid down a hail of lead, striking Miles three times and no doubt making McConnell most uncomfortable. This heated exchange lasted for several minutes, both sides no doubt becoming more and more cautious as the firing continued.

In the return fire, according to this questionable account, a ball flew through McDonald's hat. It was a close call. He also took a ball in the chest. It was equally close to doing in Deputy McDonald. This latter ball did not take effect because it hit his pocketbook.

Anyhow, in this romantic variation, McDonald ran off the frightened McConnell and Miles, sent them scurrying for their lives. In the process of fleeing, however, they stole McDonald's and Smith's horses. That left McDonald only one alternative. He ran to a neighboring house and borrowed a horse to carry him and the sad news back to Abilene (*Junction City Union*, Nov. 5, 1870).

McConnell and Miles beat a path east and arrived in Junction City about 10 P.M. the night of November 2. McConnell's hand needed attention, so they found a doctor and patched up the hand. McConnell lost two fingers in the skirmish, shot off of the same hand, according to the report. At the time of the medical care, no one knew these men were fugitives and wanted for murder. The midnight train from Abilene, however, brought word of the heinous crime.

When the original posse came together at the new courthouse in Abilene shortly after the killing, two of the men who volunteered to ride after the killer were James Gainsford, an Abilene butcher, and Police Judge C.C. Kuney. It was Kuney who, along with Smith, had just recently received the praises of the Abilene *Chronicle*. The newspaper editor, V.P. Wilson, had written that they "deserve the thanks of the people for the faithful and prompt manner in which they have discharged their official duties. A grateful community will not forget the services of such efficient officers (Abilene *Chronicle*, Nov. 17, 1870)." Now Smith was dead. And Kuney would have his killers.

When dark fell over the cold, weary posse on Wednesday night, Gainsford and Kuney continued on, heading toward Junction City. They rode on into the cold night, determined to catch up to and nab the two who had killed Smith.

From Junction City, Gainsford and Kuney learned that the men had turned northwest. So Gainsford and Kuney turned northwest, tracing the Republican River, traveling day and night, into Clay County. About 15 miles northwest of Clay Center, Kansas, Gainsford and Kuney found McConnell and Miles at a farm house. Shortly before sunrise, they were able to take the fugitives without a shot being fired. That was on Saturday morning. It had taken the two men just over two days to get the job done. The Abilene city council later voted to give $100 each to Gainsford and Kuney as a reward (Records of the City of Abilene, 1870, p. 49).

At the Kansas Pacific Railroad station in Abilene, Stationmaster D.R. Gorden was the first to bear the good news that McConnell and Miles had been captured. Gorden's telegraph key jumped to life on Sunday morning, clicking out the message that Gainsford and Kuney were bringing in the killers. They had Miles and McConnell in hand. The train would arrive during the morning.

Gorden informed Mayor Henry. Others in Abilene soon heard the news they all had anxiously awaited. The killers would be on the train from Junction City.

Some attended the little Baptist Church, some praying for Smith and some, in the spirit of Christianity, praying for the killers, McConnell and Miles. It was a solemn service. Tears continued to be spilled for Smith. Some remembered the funeral services just a couple of days earlier, the services that had started Smith on his way to the cold grave on the windswept hill at the new cemetery north of town.

Word spread quickly over the town and, by the time the train chugged in from the east, a large, milling crowd had gathered. They were not nearly as Christian in their attitude as some of the churchgoers had been. If anything, they were no longer interested in the New Testament turning of the cheek, rather they looked upon the Old Testament's eye-for-an-eye justice.

They stood around in little clusters, their backs to the sharp November wind. Many of the men in the crowd talked quietly about what the fate of the killers should be. Others were more vocal, cutting right to their feelings that the two killers be hanged just as quickly as they could yank them off the train. Throw a rope over something; hang them on the spot. Get rid of the vermin. An eye for an eye. Abilene was angry.

Some of those in the crowd remembered later that the only thing that kept McConnell and Miles from being hanged on the spot was that the crowd lacked a leader to turn it into a mob. As it turned out, few even got a glimpse of the killers.

The locomotive huffed up to the station, rolling just past it and halted. There was a cloud of smoke and the hissing of steam. The crowd was craning its collective necks for a glimpse of the two that had caused so much grief in the past few days for Abilene.

Before they knew it, Kuney and Gainsford and their prisoners were off the train and whisked away to the second floor of the Dickinson County Courthouse, just north of the railroad tracks. The killers were held there under 24-hour guard.

Slowly, cooler heads commenced directing the town's revengeful thinking. Abilene residents didn't need a reputation for their town that allowed lynching in the streets. Lynch law was not good for business in any community, and certainly not in Abilene. No matter how frustrated, confused, and full of revenge a community became, the aftermath of a lynching left a bad taste in the mouths of the civilized citizens of the community. It took years for a community to live down justice delivered by Judge Lynch.

Over the next days, weeks, and months, the legal process took hold and the prisoners were eventually brought before a judge in Abilene. How did they plead? They were willing to plead guilty to murder in the second degree. That would send them to the penitentiary for life.

But wait. There was an objection. The prosecuting attorney would not allow the plea. The public of Abilene wanted more. Sentiment demanded that McConnell and Miles be hanged. Exchange their lives for Smith's. It was only fair. First degree murder. The prosecutor would go for that.

But these plans, along with the anticipation of a hanging, backfired when it became apparent that the Dickinson County court would not be able to seat a fair and impartial jury. Everyone knew Smith. They liked him. Had been to his funeral. Sought justice—or was it revenge?—for his killing.

Everyone knew about the cold-blooded killing. Everyone had heard the story over and over. Little kids were re-enacting their version of the killing daily, wooden guns blazing, axes flying.

The Abilene *Chronicle* of November 17, 1870, told the story: "State of Kansas vs. Andrew McConnell and Moses Miles, charged with murder in first degree. One day and a half was consumed in trying to impanel a jury. Three special venues were exhausted without securing the requisite number of jurors. A change of venue to Riley County was finally granted by the court, and the prisoners conveyed to the Manhattan jail to await trial at the March term of District court for that county."

And so the Dickinson County court approved a change of venue to the District Court in Manhattan, Riley County. The killers would be tried there, forty miles or so up the railroad track, and not in Abilene.

Angry Abilene cooled some with the winter weather. Their anger and hate was draining. In many ways it was a relief to get rid of these killers. Put them somewhere else. Out of mind.

McConnell and Miles, no worse for wear for their weeks in jail, were held in the Riley County jail. The murderers were out of town, away from the streets that the man they murdered had cleaned up.

Finally, during March 1871, the trial began. James Culbertson, County Attorney of Dickinson County, and James Humphrey represented the people of the State of Kansas. Attorney's John H. Mahan, N.C. McFarland, and N.B. White of Junction City defended McConnell and Miles.

Witnesses were called and papers were filed. Among those papers was the warrant issued by Eliphalet Barber, Justice of the Peace. It had been issued on the affidavit of John Ryan who claimed that "on or about the 23rd day of October, 1870, John McConnell shot and killed John Shay [sic]."

The court issued subpoenas to John Erwin, Levi Warnock, Sr. and William H. Lamb. James Gainsford was to bring in the nickel-plated Colt revolvers that Smith carried in shoulder holsters. Eliphalet Barber, Mayor T.C. Henry, and James B. Shane were to produce the affidavit sworn by Samuel Haines in relation to the killing of Smith. T.N. Wiley was told to bring in the ax and gun belonging to Andrew McConnell.

The jury trial began on March 18 with the state trying Moses Miles first. The evidence in the court seemed to be based mainly on the testimony of McConnell and Miles. The evidence showed "that the officers in attempting to arrest the accused produced no warrant or authority; that the prisoners were in dread of a mob; that after they had Smith in their power—the officer whom he went to assist having fled—they brutally chopped him up with an ax."

According to the Abilene *Chronicle* of March 23, 1871, "This fact alone caused the conviction of the prisoners."

Miles, tried first, pleaded guilty of murder in the second degree. The judge sentenced him to sixteen years. On advice of counsel, Andrew McConnell withdrew his plea of not guilty. Instead, McConnell was charged with manslaughter in the first degree. The jury came in with a verdict of guilty and the judge sentenced McConnell to hard labor for twelve years. Both men were sent to Lansing to the Kansas State Penitentiary.

That same article in the Abilene *Chronicle* expressed the displeasure of all of Abilene when it reported, "Twelve and sixteen years in the penitentiary seem long periods, but the condemned ought to be thankful that they get off with even such sentences. Never during their natural lives can they atone for their great crime."

Moses Miles was pardoned by the Kansas Governor and discharged from prison on January 2, 1877. McConnell served until January 12, 1881. He was discharged from the Kansas State Penitentiary on that date.

So justice had been done. But in whose eyes? What their peers thought they should get out of it—death—had gone by the boards. One sentence of sixteen years had turned into six; the other sentence of twelve years had turned into ten. And Moses Miles and Andrew McConnell were walking around while Marshal Thomas James Smith, the lawman who did not believe in the use of violent guns, lay rotting in his grave. Injustice stings.

The 4,480-pound red granite headstone on Marshal Thomas Smith's Abilene grave. The bronze plaque reads:

THOMAS J. SMITH
MARSHAL AT ABILENE, 1870
DIED, A MARTYR TO DUTY, NOV. 2, 1870
A FEARLESS HERO OF FRONTIER DAYS
WHO IN COWBOY CHAOS
ESTABLISHED THE SUPREMACY OF LAW
(photo by author)

A Dying Time

November was a dying time in Kansas. The pale-barked cotton-woods had been nearly stripped bare of their big, ovate leaves. Their tiny dark-brown seeds had scattered, leaving tufts of cottony hairs like snowy down in streaks across the ground. The leaning, twisted cottonwoods now stood braced against the snow and cold that shut down tree life until the spring thaw. In a few more blustery days, even the strongest, most resistant crinkly leaves would give up and be swept away on the cold wind.

The great expanses of prairie grass lay yellowed, ready to cower and wilt under the first blowing snow. The prairie critters—snakes, insects, burrowing mammals—had already prepared their winter homes under the freeze line, ready for the stay that would permit them to live again when spring broke.

Texas cattle no longer grazed over the fields of grass. Texas cattlemen had driven their cattle north to the railhead, found a buyer, made the sale, and retreated south to prepare for another season. The cowboys who had driven the cattle north had drifted back to Texas where they would burrow into a lonely bunkhouse and wait for the high old times of spring and summer when they re-turned to the cow town called Abilene.

Many Abilene businesses closed their doors in winter. Farmers prepared their crude dugouts, filling cracks, sealing doors, bracing for another harsh winter on the plains. Planning for the cold win-ter months was on everyone's mind. Each day slipped closer to the glum, gray days of winter. Each day was closer to the dead season.

The bitterness of winter, always hard on the plains, was in the air that day. Just weeks—maybe days—from now, the snow would fly and the hot blasts of summer breezes would turn into bone-chilling knives of icy wind. But Tom Smith did not worry about that just now. Only the living wiped away tears of bitterness and sadness now, asking the painful question—why? Why was this land so hard? Why had such a good man been struck down?

W.H. Eicholtz, from Mendota, Illinois, had been in Abilene since 1869 as a "high class mechanic and woodworker." He soon became Abilene's undertaker. His other skills let him be a first class coffin builder, or he could order out the cast iron, metallic coffins. Eicholtz had the chore of preparing the dead body of Tom Smith. Like everyone in Abilene, Eicholtz had known Smith. It was not an easy chore.

A dark cloud of grief hung heavy over Abilene on Friday morning, November 4, 1870. Teary-eyed mourners wiped their eyes, grieving for the young, handsome, and honest lawman they were burying, the quiet lawman who they'd known only for a few months.

The little Baptist Church, hardly a year old and still smelling of the new pine boards it was constructed of, was an ironic place for the Irish Catholic from New York to be eulogized. As a matter of fact, it was an unusual place for a church. Just a block away, north, was Texas Street, the street Smith had been brought to town to tame. It was the place where Mayor Henry feared Smith might be killed. The place where rowdy Texans were to be subdued. But then, irony seemed to be the order of the day for Tom Smith. A Roman Catholic funeral in a Baptist Church. A lawman who didn't believe in using guns was gunned down. His handsome head nearly chopped off. A man hired to tame Texans, but killed by a New Englander living in Kansas. How did it all come together? How did fate skip across half a continent to catch this good man unaware? How did it all happen like this?

All of Abilene's businesses were closed that Friday. At the Baptist Church, people crowded in to hear the sermon. They huddled on crude benches, not at all uncomfortable. All the proper words were said. Low moaning and soft sobs could be heard, especially from the women. Teary-eyed mourners stared at the coffin, remembering their own private experiences with Tom Smith. Remembering what a good man he was and how he was so good for the town.

For those who viewed the body, Smith's once handsome face was visible under a glass. His eyes were closed; his hair was neatly combed. Mr. Eicholtz had done a good job of covering up the damage done by the murderous attack on this good man.

Once the Baptist service was over, the cast iron, metallic coffin, an American flag draped over it, was carried out and placed in Eicholtz' horse-drawn hearse. The people filed out and prepared to follow the black hearse, first to Texas Street, then to the north of town toward a rise where the new cemetery was located. Black crepe decorated the streets.

Stuart Henry, the mayor's younger brother remembered that day. These remembrances were included in Henry's book, *Conquering Our Great American Plains.* Henry wrote of Friday, November 4, 1870, "I recall it all vividly. Behind the hearse, banked with branches and flowers, walked the dead marshal's iron-gray horse, Silverheels, saddled and bridled as he had left it. Tom's pearl-handled brace of revolvers, presented to him by the community, hung in their holsters from the pommel. Crepe fluttered from hats, arms, bosoms. All proceeded on foot to do their highest and humblest honors to their revered protector. The file of people wound through Texas Street where the marshal had patrolled in such local prominence. Then across the railroad track, the line trailed through the north or civilian part of the straggling village. Finally, the concourse mounted the gentle slopes of the hill on whose breast, upraised to the sky, spread the small prairie grass cemetery (Henry, S., p. 206-208)."

At the tiny cemetery, the mourners crowded around the grave as the pallbearers placed the coffin over the empty grave. Someone draped the Kansas state motto—*Ad Astra per Aspera* (*To the Stars Through Difficulties*)—over the coffin.

Young Stuart Henry recalled, "The residents seemed much like dumb, animated monuments. No music. Not a voice could be heard. The only sound—muffled scufflings of hesitating, respecting feet through the prairie grass! From the faces of the men you could judge that the end of things had come for them and theirs. Women appeared ready to cry and boys and girls clung to their parents. The coffin was lowered. The first hopeless clods fell dully upon it. Flowers and sprigs dropped into the forlorn cavity. Women wept. Men stirred and batted their eyelids hard to hide emotions."

And then it was over. The mourners began leaving the windswept cemetery, many of them now alone with their thoughts and memories. Soon winter winds would blow cold over the town with the biblical name; soon residents of Abilene would no longer grieve for their dead Abilene lawman, but for themselves.

The grave cost Abilene $2. A plain board served as a headstone. It had numbers scratched on it. A small picket fence surrounded the grave. Over the next few years, both the headboard and the picket fence were lost in the prairie grass. Eventually, the fence fell and rotted. So did the headboard.

Tom Smith's story was done (Henry, S., p. 206-208).

James Butler Hickok
1871

According to Hickok's friend John B. Edwards, A.P.
Trott of Junction City, KS took this photo of Hickok
shortly before he left his job at Abilene.
(photo courtesy Illinois State Historical Society)

*For my preserver of the Peace, I had "Wild Bill"
Hickok, and he was the squarest man I ever saw. He
broke up all unfair gambling, made professional
gamblers move their tables into the light, and when
they became drunk stopped the game.*

—Joseph G. McCoy
Mayor of Abilene

A "birds eye view" of Abilene, KS, taken in 1879.
(*photo courtesy Kansas State Historical Society*)

Life In Sodom

The Hays City saloon was not much of a shelter against the dry, hot Kansas wind. It was Sunday, July 17, 1870. The yellow, glaring sun was blazing hot, its rays blinding against the barren, sandy soil of western Kansas. The wind, out of the south, seemed to sweep all the heat out of Texas and Arizona and blast it mercilessly over the Kansas plains.

It was one of those days when nothing was right. No place to cool off. No shade. Somehow Sundays always managed to be lonesome, especially in the barren high plains of west Kansas. The grit swept on the hot wind and mixed with folks' sweat. No amount of clothing seemed to keep out the sand and dirt. The big yellow sky looked as if it would never produce rainfall again. Most folks waited patiently for the hot sun to go down. Not only would that bring cool, but the wind would fade, too; so the night improved Hays City some. But even then, Hays City was not much. One visitor called it "a row of saloons on the Kansas Pacific railway." He hesitated, then added to its condemnation, "Having visited the place, we should call it the Sodom of the plains (*Junction City Union*, July 8, 1871)." Actually, in addition to such favorite watering holes as Tommy Drum's, Cy Goddard's, John Bitter's, and Chris Riley's saloons, there was Jim Curry's Restaurant, the Commercial House, John Bauer's Boot Shop, the *Railway Advance Newspaper* Office, and several other businesses. "Sodom of the plains?" Well, maybe.

On the barren streets this hot, summer Sunday, nothing was moving—except the wind-blown grit. Several of the saloons were open, horses hitched in the heat in the street, cinches loosened, their tails switched, eyes closed against the blowing dust, and an occasional hoof rose and stomped the parched earth. The meat market and R.W. Evan's Grocery Store were closed, it being Sunday. Those at the town's hotels were inside out of the gritty wind and heat—sort of.

Hays City was a product of Fort Hays and lay along the Kansas Pacific tracks. The Smoky Hill trail, surveyed from Atchison, Kansas to Denver during 1860, passed nearby. After David A. Butterfield initiated a stage and freight service called the Butterfield Overland Dispatch, there was a need for military protection. Fort Hays was established, but, originally, was named Fort Fletcher. The name was changed to Fort Hays in 1866. The Kansas Pacific came during 1869 and Fort Hays became the protector of the railroad.

Confrontations with the native Arapaho, Cheyenne, Comanche, Kiowa, Pawnee, and Sioux Indians had cooled some by the summer of 1870. Most of the excitement for the soldiers at Fort Hays came in town, especially on payday when the privates collected their $13-per-month salary. Or anytime they went to town and got into a fight.

Hays City grew up as a military town on Big Creek beside Smoky Hill Trail. Many of the more successful towns in the West grew up around military posts. Soldiers from the fort, freighters dry and thirsty off the trail, railroad workers laid over, and cattlemen drawn to the shipping offered by the railroad frequented the community. The smooth talking gamblers and hard-looking prostitutes who were drawn to any frontier town with money also arrived and took up residence and began plying their trades (Oliva, 1980, p. 39).

But on a day like this Sunday, July 17, 1870, all of Hays City's residents suffered the misery and heat of summer in western Kansas. Even the foul-tasting whiskey did little to soothe a man's throat or slake his thirst. It was one of those days when getting drunk didn't even come easy.

Propped against the wall, the back legs of his wooden chair taking all his weight, was James Butler Hickok. Folks called him "Wild Bill." Sweat trickled slowly from under his wide hat brim, but he didn't seem to notice it. The only time he bothered to wipe away the sweat was when it ran down his long nose. Just before a drop formed, he wiped it away with a handkerchief from his pocket. He was in shirt sleeves. He wasn't wearing his cloth coat. He liked the coat. He thought it gave him a certain class. He wore it, even in this heat. But not during the day. Shirt sleeves was his style in the sweltering heat of Hays City and Ellis County these days. On days like this, his long hair was uncomfortable. He'd visit the bathhouse later. A bath would cure all of this.

Now and then, Hickok removed his felt hat and swept his hair back away from his face. Replacing the hat, he'd glance around the table at the other players, his sad eyes flicking from one to the other quickly, looking for a hint of bluff, a touch of over-confidence, a flicker of a lie. He was a good poker player.

It was nearly too hot to play cards, but concentration on the cards kept his mind off the heat, the miserable, dirty Kansas gritty heat. He wondered why he stayed out on these plains. His Illinois home had never seen weather so harsh. But it had been a while since he had made the decisions that caused him to leave Illinois and come West. Come to think of it, he really didn't know much about that young fellow, James Butler Hickok, that he left back there in Illinois in the 1850s. Now Wild Bill Hickok was a different matter. The West had performed magic with Wild Bill. This new Hickok was forged out of gunfights, the Civil War, Indian wars, frontier politics, and sensational newspaper stories.

From time to time, the other patrons in the saloon grew boisterous and loud, but Hickok seemed not to notice. The gaudy women, their faces smeared with too much paint, laughed too loud, their yellowed teeth and sour whiskey breath nearly too much for a sober patron to tolerate.

There were men leaning on the crude bar and others in chairs at tables. They were civilians, cowboys, railroad workers, and soldiers, especially on this Sunday, especially as the sun began to settle in the west.

Hickok knew many of those in the saloon. He'd been around Hays City off and on for a spell. These folks had voted for him in the August 23 election for Ellis County sheriff just a year earlier. Elected him, too. He'd served right through until December 31 when the new sheriff, Peter Lanihan, took over.

These same folks had also voted him out of office. That was on November 2, 1869. Sheriff Laniham ran with Democrat help and won 114 to 89. Hickok ran on the Independent ticket (*Leavenworth Times and Conservative*, Nov. 5, 1869).

In defeat, though, Wild Bill got about as much notoriety as most get for winning. A Rochester, New York, newspaper announced—for some forgotten reason—that "Wild Bill has been elected sheriff of Ellis county, Texas."

Unremarkable because it was only another newspaper that got the story wrong, the *Rochester Chronicle* was, nevertheless, taken to task by the *Leavenworth Times and Conservative*. On December 10, 1869, the Leavenworth newspaper offered several reasons why the Rochester paper erred. "He didn't get votes enough," they offered for starters. "The people of Texas didn't like him for sheriff," a silly statement since Hickok had not been a Texas sheriff. They concluded, "There is no such county in Texas. Wild Bill is Deputy Sheriff of Ellis County, Kansas." The news reporter summed up, "There are other reasons but it is not necessary to give them."

Wild Bill was always good for a story. True, or not. Some newsmen did, however, get the story right on occasion—or did they?

Twenty-six-year-old Henry Morton Stanley, not yet famous, interviewed the twenty-nine-year-old Hickok near Ellsworth, Kansas, during the spring of 1867. Stanley, later to abandon the American West for the relative civilization of the deep, dark jungles of Africa in search of Scottish missionary and explorer Dr. David Livingstone, reported his meeting with Hickok in the April 4, 1867, edition of the St. Louis *Missouri Democrat*.

Stanley, a native of Wales, wrote, "James Butler Hickok, commonly called 'Wild Bill,' is one of the finest examples of that peculiar class known as frontiersman, ranger, hunter, and Indian scout. He is now thirty-eight years old, and since he was thirteen the prairie has been his home. He stands six feet one inch in his moccasins, and is as handsome a specimen of a man as could be found. We were prepared on hearing of 'Wild Bill's' presence in the camp, to see a person who might prove to be a coarse and illiterate bully. We were agreeably disappointed however. He was dressed in fancy shirt and leathern leggings. He held himself straight, and had broad, compact shoulders, was large chested, with small waist, and well-formed muscular limbs. A fine, handsome face, free from blemish, a light mustache, a thin pointed nose, bluish-grey eyes, with a calm look, a magnificent forehead, hair parted from the center of the forehead, and hanging down behind the ears in wavy, silken curls, made up the most picturesque figure. He is more inclined to be sociable than otherwise; is enthusiastic in his love for his country and Illinois, his native State; and is endowed with extraordinary power and agility, whose match in these respects it would be difficult to find. Having left his home and native State when young, he is a thorough child of the prairie, and inured to fatigue. He has none of the swaggering gait, or the barbaric jargon ascribed to the pioneer by the Beadle penny-liners. On the contrary, his language is as good as many a one that boasts 'college larning.' He seems naturally fitted to perform daring actions. He regards with the greatest contempt a man that could stoop low enough to perform 'a mean action.' He is generous, even to extravagance. He formerly belonged to the 8th Missouri Cavalry (Stanley, p. 5-8)."

Stanley managed to get some of the story right.

But by July 17, 1870, young Stanley and his prolific pen had long since left Kansas. He wrote accounts of events from Europe, the Middle East, India, and Africa, where in November 1871,

Stanley arrived at Ujiji on Lake Tanganyika and found Dr. Livingstone who had been incommunicado for four years.

Hickok had been away from Hays City since January 1870. A July visit back to his old stomping grounds seemed to be in order. It was while on this visit that Hickok and the U.S. Army had a disagreement. Whether the events of the evening of July 17, 1870, had anything to do with that is not certain. As a matter of fact, the events of July 17, 1870, have very little certainty about them.

The blistering sun was gone now and the breathless night was on them. The dim kerosene lights in Thomas Drum's saloon seemed to cool the night some. The wind was done for the day. The card game had gone on until about 9:30 P.M., but one of the players quit, and another, and another.

Hickok now stood at the bar, passing the time talking to the bartender. Two soldiers, wearing light blue trousers trimmed with yellow cavalry stripes and navy blue blouses, stepped through the front door. Both men wore the familiar kepi, or forage cap. Both men had pistols slipped inside their wide black belts.

Neither Hickok nor the bartender paid any attention to the soldiers. They were obviously over from Fort Hays, a couple of miles away. They'd come out after 9:30 tattoo roll call. A little fun, a little whiskey, and they'd return to post before the first call for reveille sounded at 5:45 A.M. They'd not be in much shape for work details, but stable call wasn't until 7 A.M. and they'd catch a nap before then.

These two men didn't know it at the time, but when they stepped through the door to Drum's Saloon, they also stepped into the pages of history. Both men were privates, members of the 7th U.S. Cavalry, the unit that Custer's errors and the Sioux and Cheyenne Indians were going to make famous in a half-dozen years. Joseph G. Rosa's outstanding research in compiling information for *They Called Him Wild Bill: The Life and Adventures of James Butler Hickok*, has cut through myth and the National Archives to identify these two Fort Hays cavalrymen as Pvt. Jerry Lonergan and Pvt. John Kile.

Lonergan, born in Ireland about 1841, joined Company M of the 7th Cavalry on December 26, 1867, in New York. He was a burly man. A sergeant from the 7th who remembered Lonergan called him "powerful" and a "pugilist."

John Kile was a native of Troy, New York, and about five years younger than Lonergan. Kile had enlisted in an infantry outfit in 1867, was discharged the next year, and joined Company I of the 7th in May 1870. He hadn't seen much of Hays City, nor would he.

Lonergan spotted Hickok, the long curly hair falling over his shoulders. Lonergan made straight for Hickok, Kile following. Hickok's hair style was markedly different from the short hair the soldiers wore.

Lonergan slipped silently behind Hickok and quickly threw his arms around Hickok, pulling him down backwards onto the floor. Lonergan managed to keep Hickok's arms extended straight out, away from his body.

Why had Lonergan performed such a foolhardy deed? No one seems to be sure of Lonergan's motives. Some say that the two men had words earlier, perhaps while Hickok was a peace officer the previous fall, or scouting for the Army, or just hanging around Hays City. Perhaps Lonergan had a grudge because of one of the two killings that Hickok had performed in Hays City during the previous year.

But just now, Hickok was in a particular fix. He reacted by getting his right arm loose and going for one of his pistols. This was probably one of a matched pair of silver-plated, engraved 1851 Navy Colt revolvers with ivory grips. He had guided a hunting trip for U.S. Senator Henry Wilson of Massachusetts during 1869. Wilson presented him with twin, silver-plated .36 caliber cap-and-ball revolvers (Rosa, *They Called Him Wild Bill,* p. 77).[8]

The shiny Navy Colt came up out of his waistband where he'd had it butt forward. Hickok thumbed the hammer in the same instant, but Lonergan managed to grab his wrist. The men grunted and struggled, now both aware of the new seriousness of the fight. Someone would likely get shot.

Kile had seen the lightning move as Hickok's hand suddenly was full of Colt. He felt for his own pistol, brought it out, and put the barrel against Wild Bill's ear. He'd settle this fight now. Kile had every intention of killing Hickok. He thumbed the hammer and jerked the trigger. Nothing happened. His revolver misfired. Snap. Nothing.

Hickok, still struggling, was in a desperate fix. He was going to die right here unless something turned. He twisted his wrist and squirmed about, trying to free himself. Lonergan was a big, powerful man, but Hickok was lithe and strong. By straining, he moved the pistol around to where....

Hickok pulled the trigger of the Colt and the ball tore through Kile's wrist, causing him to lose all interest in shooting Hickok. Quickly, Hickok thumbed the hammer and let fly another ball. This one struck Kile in the side, tearing its way nearly completely through his body. Kile spun as a shocked look spread over his face. Blood already oozed from the wound. The threat from Kile was done. He was dying.

Lonergan was in a fix now. His companion Kile, blood seeping from his wounds, was down and no longer of any use to him. He held Hickok's wrists, keeping him away from the other gun. And keeping him from firing a shot at Lonergan. The men continued to strain and struggle. Hickok wanted to kill Lonergan, but the big man was fighting for his life.

The desperate struggle continued, both men trying to get the edge. Lonergan strained, trying to keep the deadly pistol in Hickok's hand from firing in his direction. Then there was an instant when Lonergan's grip relaxed just slightly as he continued trying to control Hickok's long arms. Finally, the end came. The raging fight ceased as Hickok squeezed off a shot that hit Lonergan in the knee. Lonergan, naturally, released Hickok and grabbed for his wounded knee. Hickok used the opportunity to get to his feet and run to the back of the saloon. There was a glass-paned and sashed window there, and Hickok did not hesitate, but dove head first out of the window taking wood and glass with him (Gross letter to J.B. Edwards).[9]

The bartender and those in the saloon sent for the doctor and the Army. Neither could do much for Pvt. Kile. Kile died shortly thereafter. The Army lists his date of death as the next day, July 18, 1870.

Lonergan, the ball in his knee causing him considerable displeasure, soothed the pain some with whiskey. His young Army friend was dead. He wondered about the whereabouts of Hickok, cursing him as he lay waiting for the doctor.

Hickok, safely outside the saloon, ran directly to his room and fetched his Winchester and 100 rounds of ammunition. Quickly, he decided on the safest place in town. Hays City had a number of saloons, none of them very secure. If he stayed in town, they'd find him. Kill him.

So, Wild Bill took a chance. He walked and trotted to the cemetery on a rise about a half-mile out of town. He was cooler then; the sweat of excitement had dried as he made his way to the cemetery in the night air. There in the bright moonlight, Hickok settled down among the crude markers, convinced that his end was near and he'd be joining these poor souls already planted here. To avenge their fallen comrades, angry soldiers from Fort Hays would be to get him shortly.

Slowly, Hickok settled in, catching his breath and calming some. He talked himself into a calm that would let him think clearly. Be prepared.

One thing for certain, though, if they came there'd be a passel of them die. That private he shot deserved it. And Lonegran, if he died, too, he had it coming. Hickok would exact a deadly toll in the moonlight with the big Winchester. And he had the high ground.

When the soldiers heard about the shooting, they grabbed their clothes and weapons and came looking for Hickok. They'd had trouble like this before. One of their own would go to town, get in a fight, get hurt. The soldiers stuck together in matters like this. They'd have their revenge.

Now and then, there were sounds rolling over the land to the cemetery. Some noises were from the town; some noises were from the prairie. A coyote howling in the bright moonlight caught Hickok's attention. And then the shouts of angry men prowling the streets and alleys of the little rail stop they called Hays City would pierce the night. Hickok had a restless night. Surely they'd think of this place, this lonely cemetery, and come killing.

Hickok picked up noises from town over several hours. He dozed then, waking with a start from time to time. And then Hays City quieted.

They would not come killing this night. The soldiers searched the town and found no sign of Hickok. By daylight, they had given up and Hickok realized he was in a fix. He had to get out of there, not take a chance on being seen in town. Finally, he slipped away from the cemetery and to the railroad tracks. From there, he followed the tracks east to Big Creek Station. He boarded a train and decided to steer clear of Hays City for a while until matters cooled down some. (There are other versions of what happened to Hickok after the escape from the saloon. One version seems about as reliable as another.)

Kile was buried at Fort Hays. One old soldier claimed Lonergan deserted the Army and was shot to death in a gunfight not long after. If Wild Bill heard that story, he would have been pleased at such a fitting end for Lonergan.

As to Hickok, in rethinking the actions of that night, he must have realized that this trouble had slipped up behind him, silently, without his being able to defend himself. He was vulnerable from the backside, the blind side. It was the one area that his sharp eyes could not detect trouble at a distance safe for pistol fire. Hickok would have to be careful of that from now on, and watch his back (Rosa, *They Called Him Wild Bill*, p. 156-160).[10]

Undaunted Courage

Physically he was a delight to look upon. Tall, lithe and free in every motion, he rode and walked as if every muscle was perfection, and the careless swing of his body as he moved seemed perfectly in keeping with the man, the country, the time in which he lived.

These were the words of Elizabeth Custer, the wife of George Armstrong Custer used to describe Wild Bill Hickok. She met Hickok when he was working for her husband's 7th U.S. Cavalry. She continued:

I do not recall anything finer in the way of physical perfection than Wild Bill when he swung himself lightly from his saddle and with graceful, swaying steps, squarely set shoulders and well pointed head, approached our tent for orders. He was rather fantastically clad but that seemed perfectly in keeping with the time and place. He did not make an armory of his waist, but carried two pistols. He wore top-boots, riding breeches, and dark blue flannel shirt, with scarlet set in front. A loose neck handkerchief left his fine firm throat free. I do not at all remember his features but the frankly, manly expression of his fearless eyes and his courteous manner gave one a feeling of confidence in his work and in his undaunted courage (Custer, E., p. 160-161)."

But this was a more mature, adult Hickok that Mrs. Custer knew. Born to William Alonzo and Polly Butler Hickok on May 27, 1837, James Butler Hickok was the fourth of their six children.

William Hickok was born at North Hero, Grand Island County, Vermont. James Butler Hickok's mother, Polly, was born in New York. William and Polly settled in Illinois at Homer (renamed Troy Grove later) in LaSalle County during 1833.

Named after his mother's father, James Butler, Hickok had three older brothers and two younger sisters. The oldest brother, Oliver, moved to California with the gold rush. After their father died in 1852, Lorenzo, Horace, and James elected to stay home and take care of their mother and sisters on their Illinois home place.

But the West was a powerful magnet for a boy. And in the early 1850s, all of Illinois and the states east of the Mississippi were talking about the opening of Kansas to settlement. To young James Hickok, it seemed the place to go. He and his brother Lorenzo worked out the details and decided they would move to Kansas, settle on rich farm land, and send for the rest of the family. Together, they could get a new start there in Kansas.

Wheat that had sold for only 93 cents per bushel in 1851 was selling for $2.50 per bushel in 1855. As for the acquisition of land, the Hickok brothers were no doubt as confused as others. There had been many land acts by the government. (The matter would be cleared up with the passage of the Homestead Act of 1862, but that was several years away.) And just as soon as U.S. Senator Stephen A. Douglas' transcontinental railroad connected Kansas to the East and the markets of the world, prices might go even higher. The brothers would have to act fast.

From the family home at Homer, James and Lorenzo traveled down the Illinois River, finally arriving in St. Louis. On their arrival, they visited the post office and found a letter from home informing them that their mother had taken ill. The boys discussed the situation and made their decision. Lorenzo would return to Homer; James would continue on to Kansas.

Kansas was alive with all the horrible confrontations that caused the territory to be known as "Bleeding Kansas." Senator Douglas of Illinois had promised that Kansas would be settled by "popular sovereignty." That is, the voters of Kansas would decide whether slavery would be legal in Kansas.

Tempers flared and guns blazed as factions in the state attempted to draw up pro-slave and anti-slave constitutions. Northern Jayhawkers battled Kickapoo Rangers. There were border ruffians—and just plain thieves and outlaws—that took advantage of the lawless civil disturbances in the new territory.

Towns were burned. Citizens on both sides of the issue were killed. Squatters, speculators, and adventurers descended on eastern Kansas. The city of Lawrence was plundered. A fanatical, murdering John Brown, his four sons, and three men used broadswords to split the heads of five settlers at Pottawatomie Creek. There was another massacre at Marais des Cygnes. There were battles at Black Jack, Franklin, Fort Saunders, Hickory Point, Osawatomie, and Slough Creek. There was civil war in Kansas.

Pro-slavery advocate and U.S. Senator David R. Atchison of Missouri proclaimed, "We are playing for a mighty stake. If we win, we carry slavery to the Pacific Ocean, if we fail we lose Missouri Arkansas Texas and all the territories."

By 1859, things had begun to quiet down, but minor skirmishes and acts of violence continued until the outbreak of the Civil War. Kansas was not a safe place for a young man of 18 or so. Nor was it a safe place for his mother and brothers and sisters. In letters home, Hickok let them know his feelings about that matter.

In an 1858 letter, Hickok wrote, "You don't no what a Country this is for drinking and fighting, but I hope it will be different some time and I no in reason it will When the Law is put in force there is no Common Law here now hardly at all A man Can do What he pleases Without fear of the Law or any thing else, this is no place for Women and children yet all though they all say it is so quiet here if a man fights in Kansas and gets whipped he never says any thing more a bout it if he dose he will git whipped for his trouble (Rosa, *Wild Bill Hickok—Peacemaker*, p. 2)."

Not afraid of work, Hickok hired out as a plowman, plowing like he had done since a boy in Illinois. As far as hiring his gun out, speculation has him riding with General James Lane's Free State Army during the Bleeding Kansas period of Kansas history. Similar questionable evidence shows him in the command of Colonel James A. Harvey's Free Staters. Speculators say he may have worked as a scout for Harvey's unit.

Regardless, by March 22, 1858, he was elected Constable of Monticello Township in Johnson County, Kansas. In addition to keeping the peace, serving warrants and subpoenas, Hickok found time to farm. He wrote to his brothers and told them he planned on getting 160 acres. Late in 1858, Lorenzo came out from Illinois, joining his brother. Together, they left Johnson County for Leavenworth, Kansas.

The brothers took jobs driving teams. James drove stage-coaches and freight wagons for Russell, Majors & Waddell during the next couple of years. The route he drove ran from Independence to Santa Fe in present New Mexico.

It appears that the boys may have returned to Illinois during harvest time in 1859, but James was back and driving the teams for Russell, Majors, & Waddell during 1860. By the spring of 1861, Hickok was injured. Some say he was mauled by a grizzly. Regardless, he was taken to Kansas City to heal and then Russell, Majors & Waddell assigned him to light duty at their Rock Creek Station on the Oregon Trail in Nebraska Territory. At that Jefferson County relay station, Hickok's first killings would take place.

Once Hickok or anyone else acquired a reputation in the West, the fiction writers in the East generally "improved" the events in the early part of that notorious Westerner's life. The first of these "improvers" for James Butler Hickok was Colonel George Ward Nichols, writing for the February 1867 *Harper's New Monthly Magazine*.

According to Nichols, Hickok related the story of the killings at Rock Creek Station "in his own words." Hickok's version began, "You see this M'Kandlas was the Captain of a gang of desperadoes, horse thieves, murderers, regular cut-throats, who were the terror of everybody on the border."

That was for starters. The Nichols story then reported how McCanles was on the run from the "hangman." He told how Hickok'd outshot McCanles and made him mad. And how he was guiding a detachment of cavalry in Nebraska when they stopped at the cabin of an old friend. There, according to the Nichols story, McCanles spotted Hickok's horse. ("There's that damned Yank Wild Bill's horse; he's here; and we'll skin him alive!" McCanles shouted.)

Hickok, according to the story, found himself in an awful fix. "Only six shots and nine men to kill," he figured. But, in Nichols' story, Hickok persevered. Hickok's first four shots killed four men. He knocked down another one with his mighty fist. He broke another man's arm with only one hand. He was fierce in a fight.

At that time, Hickok was struck with the stock of a rifle. And then his enemies shot him full of buckshot. But that only served to upset him. Nichols claimed that Hickok told him, "Then I got ugly." Nichols related how Hickok finished off these bloodthirsty killers with his knife.

Was Hickok badly hurt? He told Nichols, "There were eleven buck-shot in me. I carry some of them now. I was cut in thirteen places. All of them had enough to have let the life out of a man. But that blessed old Dr. Mills pulled me safe through it, after a bed siege of many a long week."

So there it was. Hickok's first confrontation with odds heavily against him. Bloodthirsty killers and their shotguns had him outnumbered, but he withstood the onslaught.

Harper's New Monthly Magazine got the attention of several who knew Hickok. One was the editor of the *Leavenworth Daily Conservative*. He wrote, "Queer.—The story of 'Wild Bill,' as told in *Harper's* for February is not easily credited hereabouts (*Daily Constitution*, Jan. 30, 1867)."

Certainly, there were a number of discrepancies. David Colbert McCanles had no gang of "cut-throats." He was thirty-two years old that summer of 1861. McCanles was educated and often quoted Scripture and recited poetry from Burns and Shakespeare.

David McCanles was an early Hickok victim. The killing took place near Fairbury in southeast Nebraska at a place called Rock Creek Station. Hickok was 24 at the time.
(Photo courtesy Nebraska State Historical Society)

From North Carolina, McCanles had served eight years as a sheriff and tax collector in Watauga County. For several reasons, he went West during 1859, perhaps to take part in the rush for gold at Pike's Peak. He was not known as a killer. As a matter of fact, he had a respectable background, one based on service to his community and that of an upstanding citizen.

Best information has McCanles growing disillusioned with the gold rush after meeting disgruntled "rushers" on their way back home. At the Rock Creek crossing of the Oregon Trail in Nebraska, McCanles found the young owner, Newton Glenn, ready and willing to sell the Rock Creek Station, which included a log cabin, corrals, and a stable.

That particular crossing on the Oregon Trail was one of the worst. The steep and rocky banks made it almost impossible to cross in rainy weather. McCanles figured he could improve the crossing by building a toll bridge. In addition, he improved the water supply with a well.

Glenn took his money and moved on and McCanles, a strong, hard-working man, began his improvements. The toll bridge was soon complete. He collected tolls of 10 to 50 cents, based on the load, to cross Rock Creek.

Freight wagons used the bridge and the stage company changed horses at the Rock Creek Station. From April 1860 to the fall of 1861, Pony Express riders changed horses at Rock Creek. McCanles had a profitable business.

Until February 1861, the Rocky Mountain Dispatch Company utilized the stop. Just weeks later, the station was rented to Russell, Majors, & Waddell as a stop on their Central Overland California and Pike's Peak Express Company, popularly called The Overland Stage Company. And just weeks after that, in April, Russell, Majors, & Waddell purchased the East Rock Creek Station. As a part of the deal, they were to make payments to McCanles.

James Butler Hickok arrived at Rock Creek Station early in March 1861. For whatever reason, he had been injured. He walked with a limp and his left arm was virtually useless. He would be on the mend for a while. There was little he could do around the station except work in the stables, so Hickok was officially the assistant stock tender, working for J.W. "Dock" Brink.

During Hickok's first healing weeks at Rock Creek Station, he met McCanles from time to time. Generally, he found McCanles to be abrasive, not someone who was easy to like. George W. Hansen, writing in the April-June 1927 *Nebraska History Magazine*, claimed that McCanles nicknamed Hickok "Duck Bill" because of his long nose and peculiar upper lip.

Anyhow, in early May 1861, Horace Wellman and his common-law wife, Jane, arrived to take over the Rock Creek Station. Wellman was to be the superintendent or Station Keeper and agent for Russell, Majors, & Waddell. He set to work in his new job.

By June, Russell, Majors, & Waddell had missed a payment to McCanles. It upset him and he rode to the station and spoke to Superintendent Wellman about it. Wellman had no answers, but agreed to go to Brownville, Nebraska Territory, and talk to the line superintendent. If the company didn't have the payment, perhaps they could pay in horses or supplies.

For some reason, William Monroe McCanles, the twelve-year-old son of the elder McCanles, accompanied Wellman to Brownville. When they arrived there, they found that the company was in deep financial trouble. They had no money, nor did they have supplies. (The company was on a course that led to bankruptcy in the fall of 1861.)

Young Monroe McCanles and Wellman arrived back at Rock Creek on July 12. Their trip had taken longer than planned because of flooding. The boy spotted his father's horses hitched at Jack Ney's ranch a short distance southeast of the station on their way to Rock Creek. He sought out his father and they talked about the trip. The boy explained that Wellman did not get money from the Overland Stage Company, nor did they have supplies McCanles could take in lieu of payment.

Later that afternoon, McCanles and his son, accompanied by his cousin James Woods and a hired hand named James Gordon, rode their horses into the yard of the East Rock Creek Station ranch. George W. Hansen wrote over sixty-five years later, "There is no reliable evidence that any of these men were armed and subsequent events prove clearly that they had no arms of any description in their possession at that time."

McCanles stepped down off his horse and walked to the kitchen door on the west side of the house. He called to Mrs. Wellman, asking her to send her husband out.

George Hansen, unraveling the story for *Nebraska History Magazine*, drew on many sources to sort out the events that followed. He wrote: "Mrs. Wellman promptly informed McCanles that he would not come out. This only added to McCanles' suspicion and anger and he told Mrs. Wellman that if Wellman would not come out he would go in and drag him out. Hickok stepped to the door. McCanles was somewhat disconcerted by Hickok's sudden appearance. He could not understand his motive in taking part in a matter in which he had no personal interest, while Wellman himself remained out of sight."

It seemed for a time to baffle McCanles, a man who did not frequently show any sign of bewilderment. Those who knew him felt that he was always in control. But, just now, he was confronted with the strange actions of this tall young man, Hickok.

Hansen noted, "Not having any quarrel with Hickok, McCanles asked him if they had not always been friends and if they were not still friendly, and being assured that such was the case, asked Hickok for a drink of water."

Hickok fetched the water, brought it to the door in a dipper. It was good water. From the well that McCanles improved. He drank. His throat was dry with the excitement.

Hansen concluded that McCanles was buying time. McCanles realized now that he had not only to deal with Wellman, but Hickok, also. That was not good. Hickok was young. How would he react to this argument that McCanles had with Wellman and the Overland Stage Company? Something attracted McCanles' attention. He looked away, then returned the water dipper to Hickok. As soon as Hickok took the dipper, McCanles left the doorway and stepped to another door of the cabin.

Hickok then walked through an inside doorway and behind worn calico curtains. Somehow realizing this, McCanles called for Hickok. He asked Hickok to come outside. McCanles suggested that they'd settle the matter, "fight it out square."

From his position behind the tattered calico curtain, Hickok picked up a rifle, deliberately aimed at McCanles who was standing on the doorstep, and shot him through the heart. Dead.

Twelve-year-old Monroe McCanles was standing beside his father when the rifle exploded from behind the calico curtains. He remembered, "Father fell to the ground on his back. He raised himself up to an almost sitting position, took one last look at me as though he wanted to speak, and then fell back dead."

From their position near the barn, James Woods and James Gordon came up to see what was the matter. They had no inkling that there was any kind of trouble. Before Gordon and Woods reached the doorstep and McCanles' body, Hickok stepped into the door and fired two shots at Woods from a Colt revolver. Wellman suddenly appeared and chased after Woods. Wellman ran awkwardly, holding a heavy hoe high above his head.

Gordon saw what was happening and ran, but not fast enough to outrun the balls from Hickok's pistol. Hickok jerked off two shots from the revolver, striking Gordon.

Wellman quickly caught Woods and slashed at him with the heavy hoe. The wide, heavy blade of the hoe came down brutally on Woods and crushed his skull. Wellman struck at him another time. Blood shot out of the wounded head. Woods died.

Wellman, feeling the power now, hurried back to the doorstep where McCanles had died. Monroe, the boy that he had shared the ten-day trip to Brownville with, knelt there beside his dead father, dry-eyed, stunned. Wellman came running up and slashed at the boy with the deadly hoe, screaming, "Let's kill them all."

Mrs. Wellman, her face twisted, was in the door watching and yelling, "Kill 'em all, kill 'em all."

The terrified Monroe McCanles couldn't understand this, this anger by an adult. They weren't supposed to act like that. The boy managed to dodge Wellman's wild swings and run for his life. He escaped, hiding in a ravine south of Rock Creek Station.

In the meantime, Hickok was tracking Gordon. Gordon was leaving a bloody trail that led Hickok into the brush about a quarter mile down Rock Creek. The others were running along with Hickok now. Brink, Hickok's boss in the stables, had fetched a shotgun. They continued on, moving from blood spot to blood spot. Finally, they found the defenseless Gordon cowering under the bank. He was gasping for air, exhausted from fear and the loss of blood.

Still, life was dear to him. He begged them to spare him. His eyes were full of fear. He was pitiful looking.

Brink thumbed the hammer on the shotgun and blasted him from close range with a load of buckshot. That was it. All three men were dead. Killed. Shot down.

Terrified, Monroe McCanles, sweat pouring off him, finally staggered into his home just under three miles away. Between gasping breaths of air, he related the horrible story of the last hour to his mother. He told her about the shootings, but he couldn't explain it.

She had doubts about all this. Had the boy gotten it mixed up? Perhaps her husband was not dead. Perhaps the frightened boy had left out some detail. Her husband had never shot and killed anyone. It was not his way of dealing with problems. He'd not have drawn a gun on anyone. Her five children, aged two to twelve, needed a father. If he were only wounded, she might be able to save him. She had to go see for herself.

Young Monroe would not go. The bloody scenes were too vivid for him. He pulled away from her and refused to return to that killing place. Mrs. McCanles went alone. Her son was correct; all three men were dead. She viewed the bodies.

Hickok, the Wellmans, and Brink spread the word that the shootings had been in self defense. Hansen, however, writing in the *Nebraska History Magazine*, interviewed Frank Helvey. Helvey and his brothers buried the three men. The bodies of the three men had not been moved when Helvey arrived on the scene. He found all three right where they were killed. None had a weapon. No gun belt. No holster.[11]

Helvey and his brothers buried the bodies. McCanles and Woods were buried together in a crude box. They wrapped Gordon in a blanket before dropping him in the ground.

What did the law say about the killings? A "trial" was held at Beatrice in "Pap" Towle's cabin. Justice of the Peace T. M. Coulter of Gage County presided. Twelve-year-old Monroe McCanles was the only witness not implicated in a crime. The court would not allow him to testify. The Wellmans' and Hickok's testimonies were allowed (*Nebraska History Magazine*, Apr-June, 1927).

And on and on the story goes, accusations flying from one author to another, causes for the killings including sinister tales involving women, money, lust, hatred—the stuff of fiction.

James Butler Hickok, still not known as "Wild Bill," was, however, making a name for himself. And the name was mainly good. The McCanles killings did not seem to harm his reputation. Following a stint in the Union Army in one capacity or the other, Hickok ranged over other areas of the West. He made new acquaintances, was asked to repeat the affair at Rock Creek Station, and did, although it became so embellished that he may have had trouble remembering the truth, the whole truth.

Hickok was with Lt. Col. George Armstrong Custer as a scout a few years later on the Gen. Winfield S. Hancock Expedition of 1867. It was Custer's first experience with Indians.

Writing for *Galaxy Magazine* in 1872, Custer wrote about Hickok. Custer was to repeat the story in *My Life on the Plains*, published in 1874. Custer wrote, "Among the white scouts were numbered some of the most noted in their class. The most prominent man among them was 'Wild Bill'...He was a Plainsman in every sense of the word yet unlike any other of his class." Custer continued:

Whether on foot or on horseback, he was one of the most perfect types of physical manhood I ever saw. Of his courage there could be no question: it had been brought to the test on too many occasions to admit of a doubt. His skill in the case of the rifle and pistol was unerring; while his deportment was exactly the opposite of what might be expected from a man of his surroundings. It was entirely free from all bluster and bravado. He seldom spoke of himself unless requested to do so. His conversation, strange to say, never bordered either on the vulgar or blasphemous. His influence among the frontiersmen was unbounded; his word was law, and many are the personal quarrels and disturbances which he has checked among his comrades by his simple announcement that "This has gone far enough," if need be followed by the ominous warning that when persisted in or renewed the quarreler "must settle it with me."

Wild Bill is anything but a quarrelsome man; yet no one but himself can enumerate the many conflicts in which he has been engaged, and which have almost invariably resulted in the death of his adversary. I have a personal knowledge of at least half-a-dozen men whom he has at various times killed, one of these being at the time a member of my command. Others have been severely wounded, yet he always escaped unhurt. On the plains every man openly carries his belt with its invariable appendages, knife and revolver, often two of the latter. Wild Bill always carried two handsome ivory-handled revolvers of the large size; he was never seen without them (Custer, G. P. 33-34).

The Shootist

When and where did Wild Bill Hickok begin to gain a reputation as a lightning fast, deadeye gunfighter? James Butler Hickok, the boy, grew up on the tall grass prairies of north-central Illinois. Many mid-1800s families on the Illinois frontier depended on the hunting skills of the males of the family to put meat on the table. It was costly to be a poor shot, not to mention the hunger pangs.

Most of the hunting was for small game. An occasional white-tailed deer might be taken, but rabbits, squirrels, and various kinds of game birds were the more common prey of the young hunter.

The taking of the game was probably done at first with traps. A wooden box, properly constructed and baited, called a rabbit trap, was a common device used by most boys. A simpler device, any wooden box, a length of string, and a small stick could be converted into a baited trap for birds. An adventurous boy could lay hidden a short distance from the box and watch as birds followed a trail of grain to the box. The small stick was used to prop open the box. A string was attached to it. When the bird or birds stepped under the box after the grain, a sharp pull on the string by the boy trapped them there. A turtle dove, sometimes called a mourning dove, made a tasty meal.

Mourning doves could also be baited to ponds or streams and trapped in the boxes, or shot, whatever was most convenient.

Quail were hunted, too. And to make money, many boys trapped in ditches and streams for beaver, mink, and muskrat.

But these were contests of stealth. It seemed much more exciting to use a rifle to take these various animals. (In later years, as game grew more scarce, the shotgun came into more frequent use.) A small caliber, single-shot rifle was a common weapon for a boy. Certainly, the shotgun was more deadly and accurate when shooting speedy game. But there were some who questioned a shooter that shot a thirty-inch circular pattern at forty yards. It just did not seem sporting to some.

Hand guns were far more dangerous and far less accurate in hunting such game. It is unlikely that young James Butler Hickok learned much about handguns during his early years hunting small game in Illinois.

On the other hand, by 1856, there is every reason to believe that Hickok, nearing age twenty, had become quite handy with a revolver. Some earlier settlers to the Mill Creek area of Kansas remembered Hickok "astonishing them with his dexterity in hitting a target with a pistol. It was a common feat with him to take a stand at a distance of a hundred yards from an oyster can, and with a heavy dragoon revolver send every bullet through it with unerring precision. He had not then commenced his practice upon human beings."

Hickok's friend, Charles H. Utter, better known as "Colorado Charlie," claimed that Hickok could toss a tomato can fifteen feet into the air, draw his pistol, and place two balls through the airborne can before it returned to earth. That accomplished, Colorado Charlie said, Hickok drew his other pistol and while walking toward the tomato can, could keep it rolling with alternate shots, one from the right hand, one from the left.

Shootist Jim Dunham points out, "Legend and fact become almost impossible to separate when it comes to dealing with Hickok the marksman. All authorities agree that Hickok was very good with handguns, but often stories come down relating feats impossible to perform simply because they are beyond the limits of the fire-arms (Dunham, p. 8)."

Hickok lived in a transition period for weapons. The smooth-bored barrel was common when he was born. He died in 1876, not many years after the rifle-barreled and the metallic cartridge came into wide-spread use. The first practical smokeless powder did not appear until a dozen years after Hickok's death. (Alfred Nobel developed it in Sweden; DuPont produced the first in the United States during 1893.) Smokeless powder improved range and permitted stronger and lighter steel for gun barrels. And there were a wealth of improvements to firearms over the next decades, nearly all contributing to accuracy, speed, reliability, and killing effect. Hickok never used nor saw these later improvements in his life-time.

Dunham continues, "It is claimed that Wild Bill could shoot very small groups of five inches or less from distances of over 50 yards. This type of shooting," Dunham adds, "is definitely beyond my skills of shooting from the hip and I would question whether Wild Bill might not have been a bit closer than the audience remembered (Dunham, p. 8)."

Hickok's friend, Charles Gross, saw Hickok shoot one day after they'd been fishing. Gross remembered that he put six shots in a heart-size piece of paper with his right hand. Hickok then did the same with the other pistol in his left hand. Hickok also gave Gross some advice: "Charlie I hope you never have to shoot any man, but if you do shoot him in the Guts near the Navel. You may not make a fatal shot, but he will get a shock that will paralyze his brain and arm so much that the fight is over (Gross letter to J.B. Edwards)."

Another account of Hickok's skill with a weapon came in a "Letter to the Editor" in *Outdoor Life*. Written by Robert A. Kane, the letter appeared in the June 1906 edition of the popular magazine. Kane related how he and several marksmen met with Buffalo Bill Cody, Texas Jack Omohundro and Wild Bill Hickok to discuss shooting and shooting methods. Kane wrote:

Mr. Hickok treated us with great courtesy, showed us his weapons, and offered to do a little shooting for us if it could be arranged for outside the city limits. Accordingly the early hours of the afternoon found us on our way to the outskirts of the city. Mr. Hickok's weapons were a pair of beautifully silver plated S. A. .44 Colt revolvers. Both had pearl handles and were tastefully engraved. He also had a pair of Remington revolvers of the same caliber. The more showy pair of Colts were used in his stage performance. On reaching a place suitable for our purpose, Mr. Hickok proceeded to entertain us with some of the best pistol work which it has ever been my good fortune to witness.

Standing on a railroad track, in a deep cut, his pistols cracking with the regularity and cadence of the ticking of an old house clock, he struck and dislodged the bleaching pebbles sticking in the face of the bank at a distance of 15 yards.

Standing about 30 feet from the shooter, one of our party tossed a quart can in the air to a height of about 30 feet. This was perforated three times before it reached the ground, twice with the right and once with the left hand.

Standing midway between the two telegraph poles he placed a bullet in one of them then wheeled with the same weapon planted another in the second. Telegraph poles in his country run about thirty to the mile, or 176 feet distant from each other.

Two common bricks were placed on the top board of a fence, about two feet apart and about 15 yards from the shooter. These were broken with two shots fired from the pistol in either hand, the reports so nearly together that they seemed but one.

His last feat was to me the most remarkable of all: A quart can was thrown by Mr. Hickok himself, which dropped about 10 or 12 yards distant. Quickly whipping out his weapons, he fired alternately with right and left. Advancing a step with each shot, his bullets striking the earth just under the can he kept it in continuous motion until his pistols were empty (*Outdoor Life*, June, 1906)."[12]

The .36 Caliber Colt Navy Model 1851, a well-balanced percussion ignition six-shooter revolver, was Hickok's weapon of choice during most of his gun fighting days. The Colt Navy could be drawn quickly and cocked easily. When firing either a soft lead ball or a conical bullet, the .36 caliber delivered a killing blow. The lightweight pistol did not recoil or cause difficulty in staying on a target.

For shooting accuracy, any cap and ball pistol had to be carefully loaded, the barrel cleaned, and the cylinders packed with grease after loading. For a gunman to then fire the weapon with killing effect, especially at a target that was shooting back, an entirely new set of rules were called into use.

Did Wild Bill Hickok understand and use those rules? There is still a considerable debate about that. George Hansen, who investigated the McCanles shooting, was of the opinion that Hickok played by no rules—or at least, with his own set of rules. Hansen concluded as to Hickok's rules, "I have been unable to find one single authentic instance in which he fought a fair fight (*Nebraska History Magazine*, Apr-June, 1927)."

Following service in the Union Army during the Civil War, Hickok was living in Springfield, Missouri. He had operated in that general area for much of the war. Rather than being assigned to an infantry or cavalry unit, best information shows Hickok working as a teamster, something he'd done for Russell, Majors & Waddell. There are some documents that suggest he also served as a spy, sharpshooter and scout. Several documents indicate that he was a special policeman for the provost marshal's office of the Union District of Southwest Missouri.

Anyhow, by July 1865, with the Civil War over, Hickok was located at Springfield. On July 27, 1865, the Springfield *Missouri Weekly Patriot* reported:

David [Davis] Tutt, of Yellville, Ark., was shot on the public square, at 6 o'clock P.M., on Friday last by James B. Hickok, better known in Southwest Missouri as "Wild Bill." The difficulty occurred from a game of cards. Hickok is a native of Homer, LaSalle county, Ills., and is about twenty-six years of age. He had been engaged since his sixteenth year, with the exception of about two years, with Russell, Majors & Waddill, in Government service, as scout, guide, or with exploring parties, and has rendered most efficient and signal service to the Union cause, as numerous acknowledgments from the different commanding officers with whom he has served will testify.

The gunfight, if there was one, took place in late afternoon, July 21, 1865, a Friday, in Market Square in Springfield, Missouri. Hickok shot and killed Davis K. Tutt whose home was in Yellville, Arkansas, almost one hundred miles south of Springfield.

Hickok had a room at the Lyon House, also known as the Old Southern Hotel. The hotel was located on the east side of South Street about one block from the public square. Some say Hickok had a disagreement over a card game, or games, with Tutt. Others tie a girl into the story, not an uncommon twist when explaining away Hickok's quarrels.[13]

Tutt, in his mid twenties, was shot once by Hickok. He was killed. The next day, July 22, Hickok was arrested and charged with "killing." Two days later, the courts reduced the charge to "manslaughter." Hickok was released on a bail of $2,000.

On August 3, in a hearing before the court, Hickok pleaded "not guilty." Defending Hickok was Colonel John Smith Phelps. Born in Simsbury, Connecticut, Phelps became a lawyer during his 21st year. He moved to Springfield, Missouri, two years later. Phelps enjoyed a career in politics, being elected to the House of Representatives from Missouri for eighteen consecutive years.

At the outbreak of the Civil War, Phelps returned to Missouri and formed a regiment which fought at Pea Ridge in Arkansas in March, 1862. But his military career was soon over. He was appointed military governor of Missouri by President Abraham Lincoln, a position that he held until forced to resign for health reasons. By 1865, he was back practicing law in Springfield. (He was later elected governor of Missouri.)

The prosecutor was Colonel Robert W. Fyan, state's attorney of the 14th Judicial District. The newspapers of the time lauded Fyan's efforts. "It is universally conceded," the Springfield *Missouri Weekly Patriot* reported, "that the prosecution was conducted in an able, efficient and vigorous manner, and that Col. Fyan is entitled to much credit for the ability, earnestness and candor exhibited by him during the whole trial (*Missouri Weekly Patriot*, Aug. 10, 1865)."

Fyan, however, did lose the case. The jury, after deliberating for 10 minutes, found Hickok "not guilty." As is the case with most prosecutors, Fyan must have felt very certain of himself in prosecuting the case. He must have felt that the odds of him winning the case and finding Hickok guilty of manslaughter were heavily in his favor.

The *Missouri Weekly Patriot* reacted to the "not guilty" verdict by proclaiming, "The citizens of this city were shocked and terrified at the idea that a man could arm himself and take a position at a corner of the public square, in the center of the city, and await the approach of his victim for an hour or two, and then willingly engage in a conflict with him which resulted in his instant death; and this, too, with the knowledge of several persons who seem to have posted themselves in safe places where they could see the tragedy enacted (*Missouri Weekly Patriot*, Aug. 10, 1865)."[14]

So there it was. Hickok had armed himself, waited patiently on the public square until the victim showed up, then shot him. Some have said that when Hickok spotted Tutt, he calmly removed his pistol from his belt, laid it over his arm, took careful aim and killed Tutt. Did Tutt fire back? In court it was revealed that his pistol lay on the ground near Tutt. One chamber in the revolver was empty.

The judge in the case was C.B. M'Afee, the former Civil War commander of the Union Army post at Springfield (Rosa, *They*

Called Him Wild Bill p. 77). The judge instructed the jury that if they were convinced Hickok shot Tutt, then they should find him guilty—"unless they are satisfied from the evidence that he acted in self-defense." And, the judge pointed out, Hickok must have taken "all reasonable means to avoid it." Or, the judge added, if the killing of Tutt was in any way "premeditated," then the jury would have to find Hickok guilty.

There was evidence that Davis Tutt had threatened Hickok in Hickok's room at the Lyon House. Judge M'Afee ordered the jury to disregard that.

Once the verdict of "not guilty" was returned on Saturday, August 5, 1865, the *Missouri Weekly Patriot* scolded, "That the defendant engaged in the fight willingly it seems is not disputed, and lawyers say—and the Court instructed the jury to the same effect—that he was not entitled to an acquittal on the ground of self-defense unless he was anxious to avoid the fight, and used all reasonable means to do so; but the jury seems to have thought differently."

It wasn't long after this until thirty-four-year-old Colonel George Ward Nichols, legend maker, arrived on the scene. Fresh from the Civil War and General William Tecumseh Sherman's command, Nichols had written *The Story of the Great March,* an account of Sherman's March to the Sea. Nichols interviewed Hickok in Springfield, Missouri, recorded the gunfighter's thoughts and those of some of his friends, and then wrote an heroic account of "William Hitchcock," as Nichols called him.

The *Harper's New Monthly Magazine* made its way to Springfield, Missouri, in late January 1867. Fortunately, Hickok was no longer in the southwest Missouri town where they all knew the real Hickok. Hickok was spared the chuckles from the local citizens as they read the fantastic accounts of his heroic deeds.

Nichols managed to improve Hickok considerably. Turned him into something he wasn't. Added to the number of men that he had killed. Sped up the gunfighter's ability to draw and shoot—and stretched the distance from which he was deadly.

Did Hickok deny all these things? Say that he was misquoted? Say that Nichols was a liar?

If so, it was not reported. Evidently, he liked the degree of notoriety given to him by Nichols and later writers of Western fiction. Certainly, Hickok rode the coattails of "the Great Rascal," Edward Zane Carroll Judson, better known to readers of tall tales from the American West as Ned Buntline.

Buntline was a practitioner of the same type of journalism. Was it yellow journalism? This peculiar—and vigorous—stretching of the truth could no doubt fit that tainted form of reporting the news, but a more suitable—and accurate—title might be "green journalism."

Certainly, Nichols and Buntline made plenty of money—greenbacks—by stretching the truth, creating news, and sensationalizing facts.[15]

In the meantime, Hickok must have been enjoying the attention. He ran for Springfield town marshal before Nichols' *Harper's* article appeared. Of five candidates, Hickok ran second to Charles C. Moss. Moss had 107 votes to Hickok's 63. James R. Mayes, 57; Thomas O'Neil, 3; and a man named Gott, 1, also ran (Rosa, *They Called Him Wild Bill*, 5).

In 1866-1869, Hickok was all over Kansas, working out of Leavenworth, Fort Riley, and involved in an expedition headed by Major General Winfield Scott Hancock that led beyond Fort Laramie into Wyoming Territory. This was the expedition where Hickok first met Lt. Colonel George Armstrong Custer.

Hickok ran for office in Ellsworth, Kansas, during 1867. The first race was for town marshal. He lost. And he lost again during the November election for sheriff. Before the end of the year, he was operating out of Hays City, Kansas.

The next year, 1868, found him at work for the U.S. government. He hired on as a deputy U.S. Marshal and transported federal prisoners and served as a guide for U.S. cavalry units stationed at Fort Hays.

In 1869, Hickok spent time in Hays City where he was sheriff for a time. He also acted as deputy U.S. Marshal during the year. And it was the night of August 24, 1869, that Hickok killed another man. The mortality schedule of the U.S. Census for 1870 shows that in August 1869, "John Murphy (Mulrey?)," age twenty-five, born in New York, was shot and killed at Hays City. He was a soldier.

Little has been recorded of this fight. The Leavenworth, Kansas, *Times and Conservative* reported on August 26, 1869, "J. B. Hickok (Wild Bill) shot one Mulrey at Hays Tuesday. Mulrey died yesterday morning. Bill has been elected sheriff of Ellis County."

Another Leavenworth paper, the *Daily Commercial*, fleshed out the story some: "Bill Hitchcock, while attempting to preserve peace among a party of intoxicated roughs, or 'wolves,' shot a man named Bill Melvin through the neck and lungs. Melvin is still living, but the doctors say, with no hopes of recovery. He attempted to shoot several citizens, and was determined to quarrel with every one whom he met, using his revolver freely, but fortunately injuring no one (Leavenworth *Daily Commercial*, Aug 23, 1869)."

The second killing at Hays by Hickok involved a man named Samuel Straughn, or Strawhim, according to the 1870 mortality schedule of the U.S. Census. Straughn was aged twenty-eight. He was an Illinois-born teamster. The trouble was on Fort Street at Jim Bitter's Leavenworth Beer Saloon. The newspaper account from the Leavenworth *Commercial*, September 27, 1869, told the story: "About twelve o'clock last night a difficulty occurred between a party of roughs and the proprietor. Policemen Hickok and Ranahan (Deputy Sheriff Peter Lanihan?) interfered to keep order, when remarks were made against Hickok—Wild Bill. In his efforts to preserve order, Samuel Stringham was shot through the head by him, and instantly killed. Justice Joyce held an inquest on the body to-day, six well-known citizens being selected for the jurors. The evidence in one or two instances was very contradictory. The jury returned a verdict to the effect that Samuel Stringham came to his death from a pistol wound at the hands of J.B. Hickok, and that the shooting of said Stringham was justifiable."

Hickok's stint as sheriff of Ellis County would end before the end of 1869. He lost the November 2, 1869, election bid by a vote of 114 to 89. His deputy, Peter Lanihan, a Democrat, won the election (Leavenworth *Times and Conservative*, Nov. 5, 1869).

Hickok worked some during 1870 at the position of deputy U.S. Marshal (Rosa, *They Called Him Wild Bill*, p. 86), but it would be several months before the job of city marshal of Abilene would beckon him.

Cowboys, Longhorns, and Wild Bill

A woman arriving in Abilene, Kansas, during 1871, took the time to write down her feelings on entering the wild and woolly cow town. "As the train came in sight of the town," she began, "a lonesome feeling I shall never forget came over me. The country and town looked so different from the East where every farm had its wood lot, and I had never seen a prairie before. I was almost terrified with fear of what we would find in this wild western country which was settled with cow boys, long horns and such men as Wild Bill... (Stratton, p. 207)."

Yes, indeed. Abilene still had all three—cowboys, longhorns, and Wild Bill. Since April 1871, James Butler Hickok, better known as Wild Bill, was the chief of police, the city marshal of Abilene, Kansas (Jameson, p. 23).[16]

This woman, Mrs. Florence Bingham, made her home in Abilene in 1871, living north of the tracks with Mr. Bingham. A first cousin to Elizabeth Custer, Mrs. Bingham remembered, "Because of the long-horned Texas cattle it was not safe for anyone to walk except near the stores. Usually two women walked together on the streets and were never molested if they behaved themselves."

And life was plenty exciting. She wrote, "One morning a man was found murdered along the railroad tracks. The men suspicioned another man and that evening they searched him and found part of the murdered man's clothing and his money so they forthwith took this man to the creek a little northwest of our house and hung him to a beam of the old mill."

Later in the day, when the school kids found out about the hanging, they ran out to the mill to see the corpse. The body was still there, hanging quietly from the heavy wooden beams of the dusty old grist mill. The children stared at it for a time, giggling nervously, not quite understanding what it all meant. Then someone got a stick and touched the deceased's shoes. That done, the boys stepped back and stood staring. Then after a while, another boy, taller than the first, stepped forward and cautiously touched the dead man's shoes with his hand. Then, in the words of Mrs. Bingham who saw all this, the boy "swung him back and forth by his toes."

Mrs. Bingham, after living in Abilene for a time, approved of Wild Bill's conduct. She removed him from the category of "cow boys, long horns and such men as Wild Bill."

Life in the West was hard; law enforcement was a difficult mission. One made compromises after learning the trials and tribulations of living in the western United States. Did that influence Mrs. Bingham in her change of attitude toward Wild Bill Hickok, the man she'd included in her fears of "cowboys, longhorns and such men as Wild Bill?"

Perhaps so. She wrote later, "Wild Bill was one of the finest-looking men you ever saw on horseback and always a perfect gentleman as far as we were concerned (Stratton, p. 208)."

And how did James Butler Hickok get hired by the Abilene city council in April 1871? Several factors influenced his hiring. On April 3, a heated municipal election ended with Joseph G. Mc-Coy being elected mayor over H.H. Hazelett. For a number of reasons, McCoy was in financial trouble. In April 1870, he sold his Great Western Stockyards to E.H. Osborn. By the summer of 1871, John Freeland was operating the stockyards (Jameson, p. 19). His financial woes included legal battles with the Kansas Pacific Railroads. He even sold his home north of the tracks to Thomas Kirby.

Despite these concerns, Mayor McCoy's major problem was to replace Tom Smith who had died the previous November. Abilene needed a lawman. Abilene's cattle summer, the annual coming of herds and cattlemen from Texas, required that McCoy act fast. Word spread. Townspeople asked, who would be hired to keep the peace? Finally, one afternoon late in March at the Drover's Cottage, McCoy talked it over with his friend, Charles Gross, a room clerk at the hotel. (Some identify Gross as McCoy's bookkeeper.) He told McCoy he had a solution. He said McCoy ought to hire Wild Bill Hickok. Gross claimed that he had known Hickok when they both lived in Illinois. They had worked together on a farm near Tiskilwa, Illinois. Hickok had experience as a lawman, most recently as sheriff of Ellis County. Eventually, Gross and McCoy agreed on Wild Bill Hickok for law and order in Abilene. McCoy authorized Gross to locate Hickok.

A few days later, Gross found Hickok at Fort Harker, just outside Ellsworth, Kansas, on the north bank of the Smoky Hill River. There is some confusion, however, over just how Hickok got the job of Abilene lawman. Some say he sought the job, came to Abilene looking for the it. Others agree with the version above, that Gross and McCoy discussed him and invited him back to Abilene (Edwards,).

Since Tom Smith's death, there had been policemen in Abilene. Patrick Hand, an Abilene gunsmith, had the job for a while. James H. McDonald, the Canadian who rode out with Smith to deliver the warrant, continued as a policeman. Records show that the city council voted McDonald pay of $150 on April 1, 1871 "for services as policeman (Records of the City of Abilene, Mar 23, 1871)." Later in the month, McDonald was appointed street commissioner.

On April 11, 1871, Gross brought Hickok to Mayor McCoy's office. They discussed Hickok becoming the marshal of Abilene. Hickok's past was probably a topic. Finally, McCoy and Hickok agreed to meet again on the fifteenth. The Abilene city council would meet and determine whether to employ Hickok on that date.

On April 15, 1871, Hickok became the law in Abilene. The council voted that Hickok be paid $150 a month and that he be paid 25 percent of all fines (Abilene *Chronicle*, May 18, June 8, June 22, 1871). Just over two months later, on June 28, at the council meeting, it was voted to give Hickok 50 cents for every unlicensed dog that he killed. Some say that Hickok's income averaged over $300 a month.

Marshal Hickok's duties started out simply enough. He was able to size up the town, get to know some of the local citizens, and, especially, find out where the best gambling games were located. No one seemed to mind the city marshal playing poker. And the games of chance were where folks were.

Other businesses—besides gambling houses—sprang up around Abilene. The *Dickinson County Chronicle* got its start on the north side of the railroad tracks in the same building as the Twin Livery Stable. Vear P. Wilson, a printer from Ohio, was the editor. Other expansion north of the tracks, except for McCoy's spacious home, came in the fall of 1870. Late that year, the county courthouse and the jail were constructed at the northwest corner of what became Broadway and Second Street. They were made of brick and stone.

It took a while for houses to start going up north of the tracks, but when they did, they were small. In the backyard there was usually an outhouse. Some yards included a hand-dug well or cistern. Gutters on the houses and cisterns collected water. Others, in poorer times, got their water from a nearby creek or stream.

Farmers from the East were attracted to the lushness of the tall grass prairies. For many Abilene businesses, the local farmers were their main customers. Early on, men from the East decided that if the grasslands could grow such tall grass, why not try to grow wheat? The best bottomland in Dickinson County that summer of

1870 was selling for $2.50 to $3.00 an acre. Cattlemen and their herds were not the only ones attracted to Kansas that summer.

The Drover's Cottage, built by Joseph McCoy, eventually got the magnificent third story that McCoy planned for it. Painted yellow with green trim, it attracted visitors to town and offered a fine dining room and grand lounges. To keep out the hot Kansas sun, the windows had green Venetian blinds. The broad verandah offered shade for those eager to get out of the Kansas sun.

Besides the Drover's Cottage, which sold for $12,000 in the fall of 1870, there was the Merchant Hotel on Texas Street between Cedar and Buckeye. It was on the south side of Texas Street and not as large or as striking as the Drover's Cottage, but adequate for the times. Any frontier town wanting to attract business and grow had to have a hotel. Two or more hotels were better. Two men named Kerney and Guthrie had built the frame building early in 1870 to be ready for the cattle trade when it arrived in the spring. Known by several names, the Merchant Hotel was considered no better than a third-rate hotel for the cowboys.

In addition, Abilene had ten boarding houses, five general or dry goods stores, and two other hotels besides the Drover's Cottage and the Merchant Hotel during that summer of 1870. And there were saloons scattered along Texas Street, most of them false-fronted buildings made of wood that was unpainted and graying in the Kansas weather. Among them were the Pearl, the Old Fruit, the Alamo, and the Lone Star.

Surprisingly, one of the first official duties that Hickok was faced with was mild compared to dealing with hardened gunfighters. At a meeting of the city council, he was ordered to force an unwilling councilman to attend the regular council meeting. The issue of saloon license fees triggered the problem. Two of the councilmen, Samuel Carpenter and Dr. Lucius Boudinot, wanted a moderate $100 license fee. G.L. Brinkman and W.H. Eicholtz favored a $200 fee. Councilman S.A. Burroughs called for a $500 fee. Considered outrageous, this amount was the maximum under Kansas law (Dykstra, p. 126). The matter was left unsettled.

There was another meeting that resolved nothing. Then on May 8, the original supporters of the $100 saloon license fee resigned. Burroughs, a lawyer and the original supporter of a $500 license fee for saloon keepers, walked out of the meeting. That left the unsettled council without a quorum. After a few moments of angry deliberation, Councilman G.L. Brinkman ordered Marshal Hickok to fetch lawyer Burroughs. Bring him back to this meeting, Brinkman insisted.

Understand now, this issue had been flaring since the election of a month earlier. The matter needed settling. Resolved. Once and for all.

Hickok did as he was told and followed Councilman Brinkman's order. When Hickok found the lawyer, he explained that Brinkman had sent him to bring Burroughs back to the council meeting. They needed a quorum. Without him, Burroughs, there was no quorum.

Burroughs and Hickok walked the short distance to where the council met. The two men entered the meeting room. Seconds, and a few angry words later, Burroughs spun on his heel and walked out the door, headed for his law office.

Again, the furious Brinkman dispatched Hickok with orders to return with the absent attorney. This time, however, lawyer Burroughs had no intention of returning to the meeting. Said he wouldn't go. Had no intention of meeting with this callous council.

Hickok took a deep breath, swept aside his long hair and adjusted his hat. He grabbed the baffled barrister, threw him over his shoulder like a sack of potatoes and carried him back to the council meeting to finish city business.

Hickok and the council received more than enough publicity over this incident. There was talk of the silliness of the illegal act performed by Councilman Brinkman and Marshal Hickok. There was no law that said a councilman must attend a council meeting. There was a political aside, a remark about the upcoming council election. The Abilene *Chronicle* was full of the incident (Leavenworth *Commonwealth*, May 11, 1871).[17]

It was about this time that Columbus Carrol's herd arrived from Texas in a huge cloud of dust. Carrol's 1871 herd contained 1,600 head of Longhorns. The Carrol herd was the first of the season (Rosa, *They Called Him Wild Bill*, p. 183). These Texans and others had already heard that the famous, gunfighter—and killer—Wild Bill Hickok was the new marshal at Abilene. Even in sparsely populated Kansas, the word had spread like wildfire.

For that element of every group that is law-abiding, this meant only that they would get to see a famous Westerner, a real honest-to-God, gun-toting hero. For those cowboys and cattlemen who determined—in their minds—that Abilene's citizens were out to do them harm, take their money, run them out of town, they saw Hickok as a hired gun. Nothing more; nothing less.

By June 1, cattle were scattered over the grassy plains around Abilene. The city decided to publicize their gun ordinance. The *Chronicle* ran the statement on June 8, 1871. It read:

FIRE ARMS.—The Chief of Police has posted up printed notices, informing all persons that the ordinance against carrying fire arms or other weapons in Abilene, will be enforced. That's right. There's no bravery in carrying revolvers in a civilized community. Such a practice is well enough and perhaps necessary when among Indians or other barbarians, but among white people it ought to be discountenanced.

And suddenly there were cowboys everywhere. They took up the rooms in town, filling the hotels. They ate wherever they could get a meal, and whatever was served them. After weeks on the trail eating calf liver or son-of-a-bitch stew, they were ready for anything. "As to drink," one old timer recalled, "there was probably more whisky drank than water, and of a quality that would make a rabbit fight a bull dog (Little, 1933)."

And did they check their guns? The June 22, 1871 *Chronicle* reported a recent incident. The *Chronicle* related how two men who couldn't read the firearms ordinance—or didn't care to—got into a gunfight on First Street. There were harsh words and a face-off. Two shots were fired. One man took a ball in the wrist; the other man was struck in the shoulder. "The police were promptly on hand and arrested the parties."

There is little evidence that Marshal Hickok patrolled the streets routinely as Smith had before him. In addition, the city council saw fit to hire Tom Carson, James Gainsford, and James H. McDonald as special policemen to assist Hickok in his duties, although Mayor McCoy was "against the appointment of McDonald (Records of the City of Abilene, p. 71)." Hickok relegated much of the police work to these officers.[18]

What, exactly, was Hickok overseeing that summer of 1871? One writer claimed that business was off some from the previous year. He wrote that, in 1871, there were "ten saloons, five general stores and four hotels (Verckler, p. 51)." That was down from the 32 "saloons" Abilene claimed in 1870 which included all places retailing alcohol (*The Kansas Historical Quarterly*, Aug., 1940, p. 249). But other businesses in the city were booming.

The town was crawling with prostitutes and the kinds of hangers-on that they encouraged. Since there was a growth in that industry, Hickok needed help to cover the brothel district of town. As a result, the council added Brocky Jack Norton as a policeman. Norton, Carson, and McDonald worked that area of town in addition to their other duties (*Abilene Chronicle*, Feb. 1, 1872).[19]

Hickok was not involved in sensational incidents during the first months of his duty as Abilene lawman. His job was relatively quiet. Until he was certain that he'd keep the job, he lived at the Drover's Cottage, sharing a room with his friend Charles Gross. Sometime in May, obviously more certain of his position, Hickok moved into a two-story wooden cabin at the south side of town.

Sherwood Davidson, whose parents moved to Abilene in the fall of 1871, remembered a different residence. He wrote, "Wild Bill had built an ell-shaped frame house a story and a half high, a little west of the present Catholic Church."

The house was later moved to the lot at the southwest corner of First and Buckeye. The house was remodeled and "when they took the weather-boarding off to make a square house of it, they found a lot of beer bottles between the lats and the siding. Wild Bill slept in the upper room and probably took a bottle up to quench his thirst and then would drop the bottle down inside the siding (Davidson, unpublished ms.)."

Not nearly as visible as Bear River Tom Smith had been, Hickok was more likely to be located at a gaming table in one of Abilene's many saloons—although he seems to have preferred the Alamo. He was seldom seen on horseback and only occasionally walked the streets of Abilene. It was just not his style.

Hickok remained always cautious, too. Several remembered seeing him armed not only with the pistols, but with a sawed-off shotgun. Charles Gross remembered the shotgun. He described it as being no more than "1-1/2 feet long." Another claimed it was double-barreled "with a strap on it so he could swing it over his shoulder and carry it under his coat out of sight (Gross letter to Edwards)." Hickok was so cautious that one resident of Abilene remembered seeing him in a barber's chair getting a shave. His face was lathered, his eyes were open, and his hands were full of the sawed-off, double-barreled shotgun, his thumb nervously caressing the hammers.

Still, there seems to have been some dissatisfaction with Hickok's job. The Abilene City Council, meeting on July 8, established a committee to assign Marshal Hickok the jobs that they wished him to do. The committee of councilmen ordered Hickok to shut down a set of illegal games called lead and brace gambling games. He was also to arrest all persons acting as cappers for the lead and brace games. (Cappers acted as decoys for gamblers, sometimes running up the bid to artificial heights.) Hickok was "instructed to stop dance houses and the vending of Whiskeys Brandies, &c., in McCoy's addition (Records of the City of Abilene, July 8, 1871, July 13, 1871)."

In September, the Abilene city council dismissed policemen J.H. McDonald and James Gainsford "by reason that their services are no longer needed." The special committee then ordered

Hickok "to suppress all Dance Houses and to arrest the Proprietors if they persist after the notification." On September 6, he was ordered to "inform the proprietor of the Abilene House to expel the prostitutes from his premises, under the pain of penalties of prosecution (Records of the City of Abilene, Sept. 2, 1871, Sept. 6, 1871)."

Abilene councilmen may have been influenced by a story that ran in the August 24 edition of the Wichita *Tribune*. On that date, the *Tribune* reported on the situation in the cowtown called Newton, Kansas, during the summer of 1871:

Here you may see young girls not over sixteen drinking whisky, smoking cigars, cursing and swearing until one almost loses the respect they should have for the weaker sex, I heard one of their townsmen say that he didn't believe there were a dozen virtuous women in town. This speaks well for a town claiming 1,500 inhabitants. He further told me if I had any money that I would not be safe with it here. It is a common expression that they have a man every morning for breakfast.

Was that what Abilene wanted? Was the shipping of cattle important enough to turn the city into a devil's den of sin?

The city council of Abilene was struggling to keep their town—and their women and girls—decent. Through law enforcement, they hoped to "clean up" Abilene, make it a wholesome town in which to live and raise children.

This attention to ridding Abilene of the lower elements of life caught the attention of Editor V.P. Wilson of the *Chronicle*. He was pleased. On September 14, he wrote, "We are happy to announce that within the last fortnight wholesome and magnificent changes have been wrought in the moral status of Abilene."

Down at the Kansas Pacific Railroad depot, prostitutes, pimps, gamblers and cappers, their clothing just a bit too dandy for the typical Abilene citizen, lined up for tickets and a seat on trains leaving for Kansas City and points east or for Denver and points west. To encourage this moral cleansing even more, the council ordered Marshal Hickok to "notify all prostitutes and gamblers to come forward and pay fines (Records of the City of Abilene, Sept. 23, 1871)."

The cattle season was heading for an end again. Were the people pleased with Hickok's work for the summer? Seemingly so. He had done everything asked of him, with the possible exception that he did not enforce the firearms regulations quite as strictly as some wished.

There were those who compared Hickok's summer to that of Smith's. Hickok satisfied the perception of many citizens as to what a lawman was supposed to be like—two gunned, fast with gunsmoke justice, feared by the tall Texans who came north to raise hell.

But those who recalled Tom Smith—his easy manner, his non-violent ways, his gentlemanly approach to even a fist fight—were not that happy with Hickok's violent, justice in a burst of gunfire approach. They had loved Smith. He was their hero. He had paid the ultimate price. He had died for the good people of Abilene and Dickinson County.

Some residents that Hickok summer remarked that they heard gunshots at night. They even suspected that there were killings taking place late at night. Always, they claimed, the bodies would be disposed of before first light.

Hickok often played cards on slow nights, hanging out at the Alamo, his chair propped against the wall, his back covered, a glass of good whiskey at his fingertips. Protect the back. And that is where he could be found throughout most of the summer and right into late September.

It was still hot in Kansas during September. The dry, dusty wind blew in the daytime, then calmed at night. The worrisome windstorms of the spring and early summer weeks were no longer a factor. Abilene's hardy citizenry had just about made it through another long, hot summer. And so had their lawman.

Killing Coe

It was October. The days were shorter now. The dry summer heat still reminded everyone how much they appreciated the cool Kansas air at night. Still too early for first frost, but most were ready when it did come. Most gardens were in their last throes. Those that paid attention to those things knew that frost to frost in Abilene was about five and one-half months. Planting in tune with their almanacs kept their vegetable crops just right.

Folks going out at night for a stroll in the civil part of Abilene often wore a jacket or wrap, but it was not always necessary. Children loved these early fall nights and it was often difficult to get them to come into the house. Mothers calling loudly in early evening were not uncommon. Sometimes it was the sharp whistle of their fathers calling them home. That was a bad sign.

The night air was exhilarating and one could hear night sounds from all over town. Horses nickered in backyard barn stalls. Cats chased each other or fled barking dogs, the caterwauling and barking all mixed up in the black of night. Those were common noises. Now and then a night bird interjected a call. Chickens were roosted and quiet. Most folks had their doors closed after enough time for the warm inside air of the day to exchange with the cool outside night air. All the myriad sounds of families were not a part of the sounds of an October night in Abilene, Kansas, in 1871.

The night of October 5, 1871, was somewhat different. Not that the folks north of the tracks heard much, but a man sitting on the porch at the Drover's Cottage or the Merchant Hotel could probably have heard the ruckus taking place down on Texas Street. Shouting. Cursing. Slamming doors.

On that night, a few unfortunate saloon inhabitants had been caught walking along the boardwalk. A bunch of rowdies, most of them Texans, all feeling their oats, drinking whiskey and hurrahing a great deal, were grabbing up the more sober fellows and hauling them on their shoulders from saloon to saloon. German-born merchant Jacquis (Jake) Karatofsky was one of their victims. Karatofsky owned the Great Western Store, a general merchandise store, at the southwest corner of what became First and Cedar. They hoisted him onto their shoulders and carried him into the Applejack Saloon and made him "stand to treats (Jameson, p. 63)." They called this a spree. Perhaps it was the cool night air that made them get their excitement up. It made men think about games they'd played on cool nights when they were boys. Running down darkened streets, peeping into kerosene-lit living rooms, and then scampering away. Not getting caught. Daring escapes from all sorts of imagined consequences. Fleeing just ahead of danger.

Theophilus Little remembered seeing the Texans, too. He recalled, "About dusk I left my office on my way home. I saw this band of crazy men. They went up and down the street with a wild swish and rush and roar, totally oblivious to anything in their path."

Little made no bones about it. He said, "It was a drunken mob. I hurried home and got my family into the house, locked the doors and told my folks not to step outside, that the town was liable to be burned down and the people killed before morning (Little, p. 37)."

There were nearly fifty of these Texas "boys" at play in the streets of Abilene, south of the tracks this October night. The Dickinson County Fair had been going on and attracted them north from Texas. It was all in good fun. Fun like school boys might have. Picking at this one and that one. All in good fun. Forcing them to buy a drink. And as long as everyone complied with the "fun," all went well. Catch the quarry; make them buy a round of drinks. Grab him up. Hoist him into the air and carry him into one of Abilene's many saloons.

These rambunctious Texans even found Marshal Hickok eating supper and demanded that he buy a round of drinks. Hickok said he'd treat for a drink. And that was all right. He didn't mind. But he did warn them to have control and not to become disorderly. They could get the drink he promised them at the bar at the Novelty, the theater managed by George Burt of Leavenworth. Just put it on his bill. He'd stand good for it.

Obviously, degrees of "disorderly" were at play in the Abilene streets that night. The noise could be permitted. The movement of fifty rowdies from saloon to saloon, drinking beer, spilling drinks and, generally, being obnoxious could be tolerated. It was all in good fun.

It was about 8 P.M. when the first signs of fun-turning-to-trouble began to appear. A man in the crowd, Phil Coe, a tall Texas gambler who had spent part of the summer in Salina, Kansas (*Saline County Journal*, Oct. 12, 1871), fired his revolver. Not at anything. Just to make noise. Defy law and order. Put some new fire and excitement into the hilarious spree. Maybe because he was a bit drunk and shot at a dog.

Coe's firing the revolver was a violation of city law. As a matter of fact, one section of Abilene's law code prohibited anyone from packing a weapon "within the corporate limits of the city of Abilene or commons." Weapons, according to this law, included pistols, revolvers, guns, muskets, dirks, bowie knives "or other dangerous weapon upon his person, either openly or concealed."

Another section of the law required a fine of not less than $10 nor more than $300 for discharging a weapon within the city limits. The fine for packing a weapon was to be not more than $75. Clearly, Coe was in violation of Abilene law.[20]

Did Hickok detect that these Texans were packing guns when he talked to them over a plate of victuals and offered to buy them a drink as a part of their spree? Probably. Did he do anything about it? No. Why? They were probably concealed weapons. He may, as a result, have decided to ignore the weapons and let the Texans have their fun. As long as they were not disorderly. As long as they did not fire the guns. As long as they did not make the noise that let the city council members, the mayor, everybody in Abilene know that he, Hickok, was not doing his job. But the big Texan, the gambler, Phil Coe was disturbing the peace. It was now Hickok's move.

Phillip Houston Coe, Jr., born in the late 1830s, lost his father when he was in his teens. Coe served in the Confederate Army in the 36th Regiment Texas Cavalry and the 2nd Regiment Texas Mounted Rifles. It was while serving the Confederacy that Coe met and befriended Ben Thompson. Thompson's biographer, William M. Walton, described Coe as "a fine, indeed, splendid-looking man, a hail fellow well met—liberal, brave, and a dare-devil."

Walton wrote, "Coe was a man who could attract attention in any country; over six feet four inches high, splendid presence, frank face, handsome as a prince, brave as a lion, generous to a fault, faithful as a woman, positive and decisive in action, forgetting a friend never, and yet could forgive a foe."

Following the Civil War, Coe gambled and eventually went into business in Austin, Texas, when he and Tom Bowles opened a gambling house. Ben Thompson became their house gambler. For various reasons, Coe and Thompson came to Abilene during the summer of 1871 and bought a saloon and gambling house on First Street. They named it the Bull's Head. According to Thompson's biographer, the Bull's Head saloon was "successful and a had a great run of custom. So much so that a gold mine could not have been more profitable (Walton, p. 204)."

John Wesley Hardin, the Texas gunfighter and preacher's son visited Abilene in 1871. Like most Texans new to Abilene, Hardin visited the Bull's Head and met the owners. Hardin remembered Coe and Thompson: "They had a big bull painted outside the saloon as a sign, and the city council objected to this for some reason. Wild Bill the marshal, notified Ben Thompson and Phil Coe to take the sign down or change it somewhat. Phil Coe thought the ordinance all right, but it made Thompson mad. Wild Bill, however, sent up some painters and materially changed the offending bovine (Hardin, p. 44)."

The city council objected because the sign was obscene. The bull's anatomy had been exaggerated. Ladies and children passed within view of the Bull's Head on their way to church and school.

The other question: Was there bad blood between Coe and Hickok? There was a general opinion among Texans that Hickok was the tool of the Abilene city council. Texans, in general, felt that citizens of Abilene did not like Texans for their robustness, their rowdiness. And the citizens of Abilene had good reason to resent the Texans. Businessman Theophilus Little, who had owned a lumber and coal yard in Abilene since March 1871, related: "Every cowboy from Texas had to pass my office as he came in to town to get a drink of whiskey or lose his money at poker or roulette. They came in by twenties, fifties and hundreds (Little, p. 36)."

Once they were in town, their horses cluttered up the streets with manure. Their very presence made townspeople uneasy since they never knew what the Texans next actions were going to be. And when they mounted up to leave town, the shooting started.

Little recalled, "The signal for leaving town at about 3 P.M. was a few pistol shots into the air, and their ponies mounted, a general fusillade all along the line, every pony on the dead run and as they passed my office, it was crack, bang, boom, of fifty or a hundred six shooters into the air."

Little said, "I soon learned to dodge behind a pile of lumber, as soon as I heard the signal crack for their leaving town (Little, p. 36)."

Certainly, the city council had been under considerable pressure to keep this sort of thing from happening. Smith had found a way to keep the peace. But Smith was dead. Therefore, the city council had hired the gunfighter, Wild Bill Hickok, to keep these uncivilized Texans in check.

But who were the uncivilized ones in Abilene? William M. Walton wrote that around Hickok "associated and congregated the worst set of men that ever lived. He and the city authorities were in colleague, and in all things acted together—whether in the murder of a man for money, or picking the pocket of a sick stranger (Walton, p. 204)."

Texans did not like Hickok, but there is little evidence that there was deep-seated hatred between Coe and Hickok. Some have implied that Coe and Hickok had a falling out over a woman. Her name was Jesse Hazel and Walton described her as a "beautiful woman, fascinating and distracting." Walton also told a story about Jesse Hazel quitting Hickok in favor of Coe. That supposedly led to bitterness between Hickok and Coe. Was it so? There are no records that Jesse Hazel even existed in Abilene. In addition, the Texans were the only ones telling this story.

Theopolis Little thought this spree was planned in order to kill Hickok. He wrote later, "For some reason Wild Bill had incurred his (Phil Coe's) violent hatred and Coe planned to kill him or rather have him killed, being too cowardly to do it himself."

Of Coe, Little recalled, "He was a red mouthed, bawling 'thug'—'plug' Ugly—a very dangerous beast (Little, p. 36-38)."

It was the roar of Phil Coe's big pistol that alerted City Marshal Wild Bill Hickok that the Texans had become disorderly. He knew who it was. Not necessarily Coe, but certainly one of the Texans on the spree. Maybe he should have broken up their fun. Maybe he should have disarmed them. Now he'd have to. And that could turn nasty.

Hickok was at the Novelty just east of the Pearl Saloon and west of the Gulf House, a two-story hotel. The Novelty Theater had opened in July 1871 and had featured such talent as opera star Eva Brent and a range of musical performances and comedy.

When Hickok heard the gunshot, he instantly moved toward the sound of the shot. Mike Williams, a special policeman at the Novelty, was with Hickok and started to accompany Hickok.

Hickok turned him back. He'd handle it. He'd take care of the drunken shooter.

Hickok could hear the commotion of the fifty or so men gathered around the corner and in front of the Alamo Saloon. He had a choice. He could go around the corner and walk into the crowd with his back to the dark. Or, he could take a short cut.

The short way to the area of the shooting was along the board walk that led to the house of ill fame back of the Alamo, then through the back door of the Alamo. He'd walk past the long bar on the south wall of the Alamo, past the polished brass fixtures, the mahogany bar, the bottles of liquor, and the nude paintings. He'd exit the Alamo through double-glass doors, walking west and onto a front porch on Cedar Street. The porch would be lit by two lamps. The bar would probably be empty since the shooting was out front. That meant that there would be no one to his back. He'd be safe there. That was the route that he would take. Protect his back.

The men were still laughing, swearing and carrying on, but they cleared a path for Hickok as he stepped out of the wide-open glass doors of the Alamo. He was all business now. His eyes darted from cowboy to cowboy, looking for that one hint that would warn him of trouble. That one hint that could mean life or death in a gunfight.

Hickok, as usual, was ready for anything. He was ready to do what was necessary to solve the problem, quiet the shooter. And if it took more shooting, then he was ready for that.

Several had guns in their hands. Hickok could see them flashing in the light from the saloon and the lamps suspended from the porch roof of the Alamo. Hickok asked who had fired the shot, his voice full of anger.

The crowd hushed. Even the shuffling of boots on the porch stopped. It was dead still. Coe was in the crowd, facing Hickok, the pistol that fired the shot still in his hand. A slight grin showed at the corners of his mouth.

Coe said he did it. Shot at a dog, he blurted.

Hickok could see his face now. In the kerosene light splashing from the saloon and from the lamps overhead, Hickok could see Coe there. He was about eight feet in front of Hickok, the smoking pistol still in his hand.

What happened next is uncertain. Either Hickok or Coe fired. In the confusion, no one noticed which one. Lead was flying. It was almost too quick for others in the crowd to react. Surprisingly, none of them joined in the shooting.

In an instant, Hickok went after his own matched revolvers, pulled them from his waist and lighted the night with a blast from the big pistols.

Coe's revolver belched fire and smoke. He got off two shots, both of them too low. One of Coe's shots passed between Hickok's legs and left a smoking hole in his long coattail. The other passed between Hickok's legs and into the boardwalk.

Hickok's shots did not miss. Probably packing the matched, silver-plated 1851 Navy Colts, the .36 caliber balls dropped Coe. In the heat of the shooting, Hickok's shots took effect, striking Coe in the bowels and passing out of his back, taking with them flesh and bone. Not all of Hickok's shots hit Coe. Some went wild, striking others of the revelers, but none seriously.

Mike Williams, the special policeman hired to help keep order at the Novelty Theater, heard the volley of shots and came running. Maybe he could help the marshal. Williams charged around the corner of the building, his pistol out. He ran out of the darkness into Hickok's view just as Hickok thumbed the hammers on his pistols to blast Coe again. Hickok's trigger fingers squeezed off two more shots. Williams took both balls meant for Coe.

Williams had just received a message that day to return to Kansas City (Leavenworth *Daily Times*, Oct. 8, 1871). His wife was ill. He planned on catching the Denver Express that evening. He'd be in Kansas City with his ailing wife in just a few hours. Instead, Williams was shipped home the next day in a pine box. They buried him on Sunday, October 8. Marshal Hickok paid his friend's funeral expenses. Was sorry that it happened. Said so. Told the newspapers. Felt badly about it.

With Williams dead and Coe badly wounded, Hickok immediately took charge. "If any of you want the balance of these pills, come and get them," he barked.

Silence. His blood was up now. He'd have none of their nonsense. A man was dead; a man was dying. All because of this spree. He'd have no more of it. Dammit to Hell!

"Now every one of you mount his pony and ride for his camp and do it damn quick," he ordered, waving the smoking Colts.

Once that was done, he looked to see who the second man was. In the dim light, he could see. He had shot his friend Mike Williams. Some of the Texans hauled Coe off the street. Hickok picked up the lifeless body of Williams and carried him into the Alamo. Gently, he laid Williams on the billiard table. Coe was taken to his cottage near the little schoolhouse.

After a few minutes, his anger growing, Hickok went through the other saloons and dance halls collecting weapons, enforcing the law that he had neglected. Two were down all because these cowboys wanted to wear their guns, hurrah the town (Henry, S., p. 274).[21]

The sun rose over a quiet, rested Abilene the next morning. The guns had been collected. Word spread. Everyone knew what happened last night. Some were shocked. Others shrugged it off. Bound to happen in those dens of sin. Others said, bound to happen when you've got a gunman enforcing the law against gunmen.

Generally, however, Abilene's citizens seemed to go along with Hickok's actions of the previous night. The *Junction City Union*, at least, reported on October 7, 1871, "The verdict of the citizens seemed to be unanimously in support of the Marshal, who bravely did his duty."

Coe lived a hard four days. There was nothing anyone could do for him except ply him with laudanum to keep the pain bearable. He was always thirsty, begging for water. No doctor could repair the damage of the soft, lead .36 caliber ball. They'd get him out of bed and set him on a pot. The blood came. The torn intestines. The shattered bone. Gut shots were bad that way.

Coe died on October 9. He was shipped home to Texas and buried at Brenham, east of Austin. This was in Washington County, the area where his father settled in the early 1830s. The gravestone in Prairie Lea Cemetery reads:

GONE BUT NOT FORGOTTEN
PHILLIP H. COE, JR.
BORN JULY 18, 1839
DIED OCTOBER 9, 1871
(*Quarterly of the National Association and Center for Outlaw and Lawman History*, Summer, 1978)

With Coe dead and shipped to Texas, Hickok was no doubt more alert for trouble. The Austin, Texas, *Daily Democratic Statesman* of October 12, 1871, expressed Texas' view of Hickok when it reported: "A telegram from Abilene, Kansas, to Mr. Bowles of this city, announces the death of Phil Coe, a citizen of Austin. He was killed by 'Wild Bill, the terror of the West,' a notorious gambler and desperado, at one time sheriff of Ellsworth, in that State. The remains of the deceased will be sent to this city."

The Austin newspaper added, "The gallows and penitentiary are the places to tame such blood thirsty wretches as 'Wild Bill.'"

The Brenham Banner, in its October 18, 1871, issue also had an opinion: Coe was murdered, they reported, "by a notorious character known as 'Wild Bill.'"

Back in Abilene over the coming weeks and months, there were reports of threatening mail, most of it coming from Austin, Texas. On one occasion, a letter reported that $11,000 had been collected so that five men could descend on Abilene and rid the world of Wild Bill Hickok. One Abilene citizen who knew Hickok wrote some years later that Coe's mother had offered $10,000 to anyone who'd kill Hickok and bring her his handsome head (Abilene *Chronicle*, Nov. 30, 1871).

George Hansen, who researched the 1861 McCanles shootings, figured that even these killings were murder. He examined court records and eyewitnesses before drawing his conclusions. He wrote once of Hickok's killings after the McCanles affair, "From all accounts of killing in which Hickok subsequently took part, I have been unable to find one single authentic instance in which he fought a fair fight. To him no human life was sacred. He was a cold blooded killer without heart or conscience. The moment he scented a fight he pulled his gun and shot to kill (*Nebraska History Magazine*, Apr.-June, 1927, p. 24)."

Night Train to Topeka

The November cold was pierced by the one-eyed locomotive as it huffed, puffed, and wheezed into Abilene. A north wind blew the steam and smoke south of the tracks. For a moment, the depot platform was obscured in the steam.

Out of an almost mystical cloud of steam and smoke walked Wild Bill Hickok. His tired, red eyes teared and he wiped the tears away. Still cautious, he glanced in all directions, turning twice to look behind him in the cloud of smoke. Five men stood together just over there, but then maybe he was just imagining things. He was so tired.

Still, one of the men was a big one—maybe 6'4". Were they up from Texas? Could they be the ones?

It was an unsettled time for Hickok after the Coe-Williams killings. Abilene resident J.B. Edwards remembered Hickok during those days. Edwards knew he was worried. Of Hickok's shotgun, Edwards said, "He cut off the barrels, down to twelve inches in length, and loaded it nearly to the muzzle with heavy shot. He then carried it as well as his pistols while in Abilene, never leaving it out of his reach day or night (Henry, S., p. 282)."

Hickok's friend Charles Gross visited Hickok's house early one morning in Abilene and recalled later how cautious Wild Bill was. Gross wrote, "To my surprise as soon as Bill was dressed, all but Coat and Hat—he went carefully to the door looked all around for several mts & then Emptied one 6 shooter. He had the one in Each hand, returned to the room cleaned & reloaded it, then went to the door & Emptied the Other one & reload it the same way. Bill used powder & Ball—We had pistols then with Metal Catridges but Bill would not use them he moulded his own bullets & primed Each tube using a pin to push the powder in so he was sure of powder Contact and before putting on the Cap he looked at the interior of each Cap now this all strange to me & new too so I said, did you get your Guns damp yesterday Bill? he said "no, but I ain't ready to go yet & I am not taking any chances, when I draw & pull *I must be sure* (Gross letter to Edwards, June 15, 1925)."

There might be an argument that Hickok was being too cautious with the cap and ball Colts, but the Boot Hills of the West were full of gunmen who didn't keep their powder dry. There was probably no sound in the world as deadly as the snap—and no explosion—of a cap and ball pistol.

For weeks, in Hickok's case that fall of 1871, the newspapers and mail had been full of threats, Texas threats against Marshal Hickok, the killer of Phil Coe, Texan. In the beginning, Hickok shrugged off the threats, but then word came that a reward for his head had been made. A reward of $10,000 or $11,000 was more than any cowboy could ever hope for in a lifetime. Everyone packing a pistol might have an idea about collecting that lifetime payday. Hickok had lived under the strain of that possibility for a month. Just now, he'd decided to do something about it and take a short vacation in Topeka.

A letter from Texas had set the stage for these late November events. The letter told of the "purse of $11,000" for Wild Bill Hickok's life. Five men were coming to Abilene to collect his life and, thus, the reward. They'd deliver the head, long locks and all, to Texas (Abilene *Chronicle*, Nov. 30, 1871).

Hickok knew the men were in Abilene, but he couldn't locate them. After five days of little sleep and a wearying attempt to locate these killers that might just be down a dark alley stepping from a shadowy corner, guns blazing, Hickok had enough. He decided to get out of town, ride the train to Topeka, and lay low for a few days. Rest up.

Hickok had purchased his train ticket. The conductor had set a step on the ground and without speaking Hickok took the step up and onto the platform between the passenger cars. The door to the car on his right was open and he stepped into it followed closely by a friend who was making the trip to Topeka with him.

As they walked to the middle of the car, Hickok and his friend stopped briefly at the stove and rubbed their hands with the heat. His friend spoke quietly and told him that he overheard the tall Texan say, "Wild Bill is going on the train." Hickok and his friend took a seat facing toward the front of the train. The Texans entered and seated themselves behind Hickok and his friend.

Hickok was deep in thought for a few minutes, then, without a word, rose and walked to a seat behind where the Texans sat. He was there only moments when one of the Texans turned, saw Hickok's location, and rose and walked forward to the next car. The others hesitated, but then rose and joined the first.

Hickok had won the first round. He and his friend then walked to the rear, taking a seat in the last car on the train. Hickok was exhausted. He had to sleep.

The engineer threw open the throttle and started the locomotive. The engine began puffing, wheels spinning, then it coughed up to speed and soon there was nothing but the even rhythm of the car swaying gently from side to side and the clickity-clack of the wheels. Hickok's burning eyes would hardly stay open.

Finally, the swaying and clickity-clacking was too much. He slept, his friend watching over him.

About ten miles out of Topeka, the five men from the station platform in Abilene, entered the car where Hickok dozed. All wore heavy coats. The tall one wore an overcoat over a dress coat. A woman from Abilene who was on the train and knew Hickok watched them carefully. They ignored her. Under the overcoat that the tall man wore, she could see his hand, his fingers wrapped around a big pistol, his thumb on the hammer.

Immediately, when the five men came into the car, Hickok's friend woke him. In a hushed voice, the situation was explained to Hickok. Hickok was suddenly alert, ready for anything.

The observant woman saw her chance and walked the aisle to where Hickok and his friend sat. She whispered that she had seen the man with his hand on a pistol under the big coat. The woman continued on, walking to the car ahead.

With Hickok awake, and the five men bunched up in the aisle, it seemed that it was anyone's choice. Shoot or not. In these confined quarters, not only Hickok would die, but he'd take at least two, maybe three, with him. But just at that time, and for the next ten miles into Topeka, no one had the urge to die. It was a stand-off.

At Topeka, Hickok stepped out of the car ahead of the men. They followed and he confronted them as they walked out of the door: where were they going?

"We propose to stop in Topeka," they answered.

Hickok's eyes narrowed as he opened his coat. "I am satisfied that you are hounding me, and as I intend to stop in Topeka," he warned, "you can't stop here."

For an instant, men's hands twitched, poised in that familiar position to deal death by gunfire. The look on Hickok's face let them know he was ready and willing to fill both his hands with the Colt Navy pistols and deal death. The Texans considered this. The younger ones saw this as an opportunity to make a name. The older ones obviously saw it as an opportunity to die—and add their names to the men Wild Bill had sent to an early grave.

It took just seconds, but the tall man and those with him retreated into the car. Hickok stepped off and watched the train leave the station, the five men visible in soft lamplight inside the car.

With the train safely out of the station, Hickok looked around him. The other passengers had stepped inside the depot. Despite the fitful sleep on the train, the confrontation had drained him. He needed rest, sleep (Abilene *Chronicle*, Nov. 30, 1871).

Hickok's problems were not the only ones stirring Abilene in the period from the Coe killing to the end of Hickok's term as marshal of Abilene. Tom Carson, somehow back on the police force, and John Man, a bartender, were involved in an altercation. The dispute ended in gunfire with Carson doing the shooting and Man getting the wound. He was struck in the hip. The word was that he had been shot "without provocation."

The Abilene City Council met a few days later on November 27. The Council fired Carson and threw in Brocky Jack Norton for good measure. Both men had previously been let go from the police force; both men had used up their "another chance."

There seems to have also been trouble brewing between Hickok and the Council. Was he attracting the wrong elements to Abilene?

The Abilene *Chronicle* jogged the memory of Abilene's citizens and council members when on November 30, 1871, the *Chronicle* reminded its readers: "The law-abiding citizens decided upon a change and it was thought best to fight the devil with his own weapons. Accordingly Marshal Hickok, popularly known as 'Wild Bill,' was elected marshal."

With that said, the *Chronicle* pointed out, "During the past season there has been order in Abilene. The Texans have kept remarkably quiet, and as we learn from several citizens of the place, simply for fear of Marshal Hickok and his posse."

V.P. Wilson, the *Chronicle* editor wrote: "While we cannot justify lawlessness or recklessness of any kind, yet we think the marshal wholly justifiable in his conduct toward such a party. Furthermore, we think he is entitled to the thanks of law-abiding citizens throughout the State for the safety of life and property at Abilene, which has been secured, more through his daring, than any other agency (Abilene *Chronicle*, Nov. 30, 1871)."

But Abilene continued to seperate itself from the cattle trade, while leaning toward farming as the future endeavor of the community. Friction developed among the council members. Theodore C. Henry, interested in growing wheat and selling real estate, wanted cattle and cattlemen out of Abilene and Dickinson County.

V.P. Wilson of the *Chronicle* and Reverend W.B. Christopher let all know that they no longer wanted prostitution and gambling in Abilene. As an extra dose of purity, they threw in a few dislikes about city hall and the way it was being operated.

Joseph G. McCoy, the man who had brought cattle to Abilene, naturally wished to continue the trade. After all, it was he who made Abilene. He had purchased two hundred fifty acres to start it all. That was on June 18, 1867. Nearly five years later, the Great Western Stockyard was there. They could load forty carloads of cattle in two hours. The railroad had built a one-hundred-car spur.

T.C. Henry had faith in Abilene. (He bought the town site for $5,000 during 1872.) Henry, later known as "the Kansas Wheat King," would become a State Senator in Kansas. His ability to lead the people in the direction he wished to go made him "the leading Republican candidate for Governor against St. John in 1882." He was selected as the President of the Kansas State Fair Association.

In 1883, T.C. Henry left Kansas behind, headed for Colorado. There he became known as the "Irrigation King of Colorado." He died in Denver in 1914. Henry's body lay in state in the State Capitol of Colorado (Henry, S., p. xi, xii).

Even though Henry and McCoy remained the best of friends, this battle between the two men was leaning in favor of former Mayor T.C. Henry. Mayor McCoy was in a loosing battle.

A hard blow in favor of Henry was struck on December 13, 1871. McCoy was out of town. On the previous day, Council President James A. Gauthie called a council meeting. There was a bit of business to take care of.

"Be it resolved by Mayor & Council of City of Abilene that J. B. Hickok be discharged from his official position as City Marshal for the reason that the City is no longer in need of his services and that the date of his discharge Take place from and after this 13th day of December AD 1871. Also that all of his Deputies be stopped from doing duty."

The council then turned to filling the vacancy. President Gauthie, on a motion and unanimous vote, was "appointed City Marshal of the City of Abilene for the period of one month commencing this 13th day of December AD 1871, at a Salary of $50.00 (Records of the City of Ailene, p. 107-108)."

So one of the first blows had been struck on behalf of farming. A $50 lawman could not tame a cowtown. Therefore, the cowtown had to go. Hickok was a cowtown tamer. He was gone.

Mayor McCoy, as late as August 30, 1908, defended Hickok to a reporter for the Topeka *Capital*. He said, "For my preserver of the Peace, I had 'Wild Bill' Hickok, and he was the squarest man I ever saw. He broke up all unfair gambling, made professional gamblers move their tables into the light, and when they became drunk stopped the game."

But there were other Texas problems in Dickinson County during that summer and fall of 1871, a season that saw 50,000 head of Texas cattle invade Dickinson County. The high cost of law enforcement and the objection to Texas cattle being pastured around Abilene made it obvious that something had to be done. In anticipation of difficulty between the agricultural interests and the cattle interests, a board of appraisers was established in May 1871. The appointees were James Bell, Ed Gaylord, and T.C. Henry. Records indicate that at least $4,041 was paid out that cattle season to farmers (The *Kansas Historical Quarterly*, Aug., 1940, p. 256).

A farmer in the north part of the county had his corn trampled by Longhorns. Other Longhorns stomped corn and 20 chickens. Another farmer's hay meadow was ruined by an uncaring herdsman's bedding down his cattle. Bloodshed was narrowly avoided in several cases. Death was threatened. Standoffs escalated into near shoot-outs. Dickinson County farmers lost livestock to "splenic fever," also known as Spanish or Texas fever. A bad situation between Kansans and Texans had grown worse in the summer of 1871 (Dykstra, p. 223-232).

During 1871, the Abilene *Chronicle* had several letters supporting first one side then the other. A head tax on cattle was suggested to offset the expense of hiring lawmen to keep order. Someone, probably Joseph G. McCoy (The *Kansas Historical Quarterly*, Aug., 1940, p. 257), penned a letter that was signed "Ibex" and published in the Abilene *Chronicle* on February 2, 1871:

> We are informed that when Abilene was first selected as a point to locate this trade, it was an obscure, dingy place, boasting of but one shingle-roofed building, the balance a half-dozen log huts, covered with dirt roofs. As a business place it boasted one little "whiskey battery," one eight-by-ten dry goods and grocery house, containing nearly three wheelbarrow loads of goods.

The final blows to Abilene, the cowtown, came in February and March of 1872. In February, former mayor T.C. Henry drew up a statement:

> We, the undersigned, members of the Farmers' Protective Association, and officers and citizens of Dickinson County, Kansas, most respectfully request all who had contemplated driving Texas cattle to Abilene the coming season to seek some other point for shipment, as the inhabitants of Dickinson County will no longer submit to the evils of the trade (Abilene *Chronicle*, Feb. 8, 1872).

They were tired of the cattle industry. They were tired of the rowdy Texans. They were tired of worrying about their children, their daughters. They were tired of the gunplay in the streets. Eighty percent of the eligible residents of Dickinson County signed the petition.

In the meantime, during March 1872, the Kansas state legislature moved the tick fever quarantine line farther to the west (Dary, *Cowboy Culture*, p. 190). The double blow—the Dickinson County petition and the Kansas law—ended the cattle drives to Abilene.

The county commissioners called for a vote on the issue on April 1, 1872. Most knew the outcome before they cast their ballots. Abilene, in their opinion, did not have a prayer as long as they based their livelihood on Texas cattle. Voters elected against the herds. The vote was 780 to 314. That was throughout the county. In Abilene, the vote went the same way, 118 to 85, although with not as much determination. Money clouded the good sense of some of the voters.

The main determiner, however, was "the evils of the trade." Some may have even stretched the point and thought about the good man, Tom Smith, who had died because of a dispute over stray cattle. Smith's reason for being in Abilene and Dickinson County in the first place was cattle and the cattle industry. Maybe he'd be alive now if....

The stinking cattle roamed over everything, ruining what crops farmers tried to plant. They trampled gardens in town. They stomped out the spirit of the good folks trying to create and nurture Abilene. The cattle industry created an economy that the residents of Abilene and Dickinson County were no longer eager to embrace. The evils of the cattle trade were something they could all do without.

In the months to come, the cowboys did as the residents of Dickinson County and Kansas requested. They turned their cattle away from Abilene. Ellsworth, Newton, and Wichita all took up the cattle trade—and suffered the consequences. Dodge City, by 1885, was the last of the Kansas cattle towns. In 1885, a Kansas quarantine law moved the quarantine line into Colorado.

Already down at the Drover's Cottage, preparations were underway. Moses George was moving the Drover's Cottage. Without the cattle industry, visitors to Abilene would be far fewer than during cattle days. He had the Drover's Cottage torn down and loaded onto a flatcar. The railroad moved the hotel to Ellsworth. There would be cattlemen there. There would be lemonade served on the big verandah. There would be talk of cattle and money.

In the May 30, 1872, Abilene *Chronicle*, editor V. P. Wilson observed: "The town of Abilene is as quiet as any village in the land. Business is not as brisk as it used to be during the cattle season—but the citizens have the satisfaction that Hell is more than sixty miles away." (Here Wilson referred to the new cowtown, Ellsworth.)

Wild and woolly Kansas began to tame down. And so did Wild Bill Hickok.

And Rumors Begat Rumors

Wild Bill Hickok's life after Abilene was fraught with rumor. There were stories of new jobs, new gunfights, and new killings. From time to time, he'd be rumored shot down and killed. On several occasions, he wrote to newspapers explaining that he was very much alive. It seemed that when a newspaper had a slow newsday, they could always sell a few extra papers with an account of Hickok's being shot and killed by a lone gunman, or several gunmen, or Indians, or some sort of imaginary combination of all of these.

Soon after his dismissal at Abilene, there was a report that Hickok would soon become the marshal of Newton, Kansas, about 65 miles south. Newton, founded during 1871, lay along the north and south sides of the Atchison, Topeka, and Santa Fe Railroad in the valley of the Arkansas River. Like Abilene, it was a cow town. Like Abilene, it had problems of lawlessness.

Like Abilene, Newton had grown up in a hurry. North of the tracks lay the false-fronted buildings of the more civil citizens of Newton. On the south side, there was the typical cow town sin city. Called Hide Park, bordellos, dance halls, and saloons were located there.

Already, Newton had a reputation. On Sunday, August 20, 1871, the "General Massacre" had occurred at Tuttle's Saloon. A man named Mike McCluskie and a Texan named William Baylor mixed it up, guns blazing, lead flying. And then the broken bones and torn flesh. Gunsmoke hanging heavy in the long barroom.

Men crying, pleading, praying—bleeding. Three lay dead. A half-dozen or so were wounded. The little town of Newton was becoming a true cow town (Topeka *Daily Commonwealth*, Aug. 22, 1871).

There is little doubt that Newton needed cleaning up. But if Hickok ever considered the Newton job, there is no proof of it. Like so many of the rumors about Hickok, this one seems to have lived and died in local newspapers.

Another cow town that claimed to have an attraction for Hickok was located at Ellsworth on the Smoky Hill River about 60 miles west of Abilene. Its boom years were from 1871 to 1873. Phil Coe's gambling partner, Ben Thompson, was involved in a gambling hall and saloon there for a while. In regard to Hickok and the town of Ellsworth, rumor had it that the local newspaper would hire Hickok as the "fighting editor" of the Ellsworth *Reporter*. Whether an Ellsworth newspaperman had his tongue firmly planted in his cheek or not is not revealed (Ellsworth *Reporter*, Mar. 28, 1872).

The best information says that Hickok left Abilene in January 1872 and journeyed to Kansas City where he stayed in the St. Nicholas Hotel. There was a modern, active police force there and he could expect protection from the tenacious Texans. In his spare time, he played faro at the Marble Hall at 522 Main Street (Patterson, p. 84).

And then there were the rumors of Hickok's death. These reports spread throughout the West and East, appearing in newspapers from coast to coast. Everyone seemed to want to learn of the death of Wild Bill Hickok. Between 1872 and 1876, his death was reported from Galveston, Kansas City, Dodge City, and various other communities.

Hickok spent some time with his friend Charles H. "Colorado Charley" Utter at Georgetown, Colorado (Rosa, *They Called Him Wild Bill*, p. 218). The little gold strike community located at an altitude of 8,489 feet had developed after the 1859 Clear Creek strike, but faded when the gold ran out. Then, in 1864, silver was found about five miles northwest and the gold bust turned into a silver boom. Georgetown, known as the "Silver Queen," soon claimed the title of third largest city in Colorado. With solidly built buildings, it had attracted Utter who owned a rooming house where Hickok stayed. Tucked away in a narrow scenic valley, Georgetown was a good place to play poker. Hickok spent most of his time at the card tables.

That summer, Hickok was offered a job as the master of ceremonies for Sidney Barnett's "Grand Buffalo Hunt." Barnett, a Canadian museum owner, put on a show at Niagara Falls and Hickok was involved. The August 1872 affair lasted only a few days and, by September, Hickok was headed for Kansas City (Rosa, *They Called Him Wild Bill*, p. 167-168).

An event occurred during September 1872 in Kansas City. Again, it was a confrontation with Texans. About 30,000 people attended the Kansas City Fair. The gala fair drew folks from all over Kansas, Missouri and Texas. A band played in one area of the fair and many listeners gathered around to listen. Finally, a reported group of fifty or so cowboys from Texas began waving their pistols and requesting the band play "Dixie."

Tension mounted as the crowd was quickly factionalized into Union and Confederate sympathizers. Just as the band struck up "Dixie," Hickok appeared out of the crowd. The September 28, 1872, Topeka Kansas *Daily Commonwealth* reported, "Wild Bill stepped forward and stopped the music and more than fifty pistols were presented at William's head, but he came away unscathed."

J.B. Edwards remembered, "Hickok was offered a large salary to go on the stage and even made an effort to follow that profession, but only for a short time. He said it was against his nature to appear before the public on the stage (Henry, S., p. 280)."

In December 1872, the opening curtain went up on *The Scouts of the Plains*, a western show put on by Buffalo Bill Cody, Texas Jack Omohundro and Ned Buntline. Buntline, who seemed to have as many aliases as he did wives, was born Edward Zane Carroll Judson in New York during 1823. He was run out of towns from New York to the Mississippi River and, eventually, settled on journalism as a profession. He worked for newspapers, but found them too tame for the kind of fiction he had floating around in his imaginative mind. He thus took up the art of hero-making. His first dime novel Western was *Buffalo Bill, King of the Border Men.* The tales were tall, the stories sensational, the heroes bigger than life. They sold like cool beer at the end of a trail drive.

Buntline decided to put his stirring stories on the stage, bring the heroes to life, prove that all he wrote about wasn't fiction. He hired some of his bigger-than-life characters to fill the bill. Texas Jack and Buffalo Bill were naturals for Buntline's purposes.

After a while, Omohundro and Cody grew weary of Buntline and his schemes and decided to form their own show. To take the place of Buntline on the stage, they hired Wild Bill Hickok.

Hickok was popular with the audiences, drawing cheers and ample applause wherever he went. He may have been the most authentic Westerner of the three. But working in the theater went against his frontier grain. On the frontier, a man rose when he wanted. He might stay up all night and sleep half the day away. That was not the case with the acting profession.

In addition, Hickok had always tried to be honest with those around him and to himself. Once during an act, with the players on stage sitting around a campfire telling tall tales and sucking friendship and conversation from a jug of whiskey, it came time for Hickok to take a drink. He hooked his finger in the handle and hoisted the jug onto his elbow. He looked at the crowd, licked his lips and drew from the jug.

Suddenly, Hickok lowered the jug, shook his head and spit a stream of liquid onto the stage floor. He yelled loud enough for all to hear, "Any damn fool would know that was cold tea." (Others claim a similar experience when Wild Bill spewed the cold tea, then called out, "Cold tea don't count—either I get real whisky or I ain't tellin' no story.")

Remembering lines did not set well with Hickok either. The plays were mainly action events, but there were necessary lines to be memorized and spoken in order to carry the weak stories. Hickok could hardly bear to speak the lines. He'd often gulp, then screw up his courage to say such things as: "Fear not, fair maid; by heavens, you are safe at last with Wild Bill, who is ever ready to risk life and die if need be in the defense of weak and helpless womanhood (Monaghan, p. 29-32)."

Well, it was enough to make a grown man weep. He'd rather go bear hunting with a switch. Skin a wildcat. Wrestle a cougar.

In addition to this unmanly embarrassment, Hiram Robbins, manager of the Buffalo Bill troupe, also noted, "Wild Bill's actual merits made him a reputation, but with all of his daring exploits, which he modestly attempted to keep in the back-ground, he was not so well-known throughout the country as Cody."

Robbins made another point about Hickok. He wrote, "I found it was necessary to assign Wild Bill, the actual hero, to a minor part, on account of his effeminate voice. Although he was a large and powerful man, he had a voice like a girl, altogether too weak for the part which he would naturally take."

E.C. Little, a citizen of Abilene, noted the same quality in Hickok: "There were certain traits of his character strangely enough almost womanly." On the contrary, Leander P. Richardson writing in *Scribner's Monthly* Magazine during February 1877, claimed that Hickok's "voice was low and musical (*Scribner's Monthly*, Feb., 1877)."

It was just a matter of time before Hickok had his fill of discomfort over this play-acting. Before the season ended, Hickok told Hiram Robbins that he was leaving and asked him to give Cody a message: "Tell that long-haired son-of-a-gun I have no more use for him and his damned show business (Monaghan, p. 32)."

With show business, it has always been difficult to sort fact and fiction, corral them, pen them down. The March 14, 1874, *Rochester Democrat and Chronicle* had a headline:

WILD BILL
HE LEAVES TROUPE
FOR THE WESTERN FRONTIER

The word was that General Philip Sheridan had called Hickok back to the frontier to join the Army at Fort Laramie. There was an urgency about the matter. Surely, some thought, there must be an emergency that calls Hickok back to the frontier. Are the Indians on the warpath?

If there was an emergency, there is no proof of it.

Some said Hickok might start up his own show. It would be an outdoor show with horses and buffalo. The people wanted action. There would be no room in his show, according to the rumors, for this sitting around on a stage, drinking tea out of a jug. But the Hickok show never happened.

Late in 1874, Hickok accompanied a hunting party that newspapers of the day claimed was from England. The year 1872 had been a popular one for foreigners coming to the wild West to hunt. In the fall of 1871, the Grand Duke Alexis of Russia, the third son of Czar Alexander II, boarded a ship, with a Russian battle fleet for an escort, and came to America. Alexis let it be known that he wished to visit the prairies of the American West and "see a body of American Indians and observe the manner in which they killed buffaloes."

Learning of this, General Philip Sheridan began making plans to accommodate the Grand Duke. Buffalo Bill Cody became the obvious choice to conduct this gala event. Sheridan sent Cody to find the Brule Sioux and their headman Spotted Tail. Spotted Tail thought all this a grand idea and said he'd choose on hundred of his people to come along on the hunt.

In the meantime, the Army set up a camp at Red Willow Creek, south of Fort McPherson, located on the south bank of the North Platte in Nebraska, near the Oregon Trail. By the time Grand Duke Alexis arrived by train during January 1872, "Camp

Alexis" was equipped with heated tents that had wooden and carpeted floors.

Alexis enjoyed a Sioux war dance and hunted buffalo. Riding Buckskin Joe, Cody's favorite buffalo horse, Alexis managed to kill eight buffalo while in America.

For the summer of 1874, the experienced Cody had, according to the newspapers, hired out to English hunters. They had also hired Wild Bill Hickok as a guide. The Denver *Rocky Mountain News* of July 31, 1874 reported: "Those English millionaire hunters, with 'Buffalo Bill' and 'Wild Bill' for guides, who came out here to out-do the sporting achievements of the Grand Duke Alexis, took the saddle last Monday, and by this time have fairly commenced the extermination of all the wild game in the Platte valley. Major Moore, with a company of cavalry, has gone out with the party, merely to keep the Englishmen from destroying the redskins, while exterminating the buffaloes (Rosa, *They Called Him Wild Bill*, p. 273)."[22]

But Hickok was home. On the frontier. Where he had headed two decades earlier when he left north-central Illinois for Kansas. Newspaper accounts had him in Cheyenne, Denver, back to Kansas City, then to Colorado, and Wyoming again. The frontier was where he belonged, where he desired to be. Abilene's J.B. Edwards remarked once of Hickok, "He could not keep away from the border, and when Deadwood was booking its first boom in the Black Hills in '73 or '74, he drifted there... (Henry, S., p. 280)."

The Killing Time

L ife plays strange tricks. James Butler Hickok seems at once to have been involved with many women and not involved with any women. Nearly every time that he was involved in a gunfight or killing, suspicions flew that the shootings somehow involved a woman. Yet solid proof of this involvement, this woman, seldom became public knowledge.

One woman, Martha Jane Cannary, or Canary, known as Calamity Jane, claimed she knew Hickok, but she was guilty on several occasions of seeking out publicity. A *Cheyenne Daily Leader* editor claimed she once ordered him to run the following note in the paper: "Print in the *Leader* that Calamity Jane, the child of the regiment and a pioneer white woman of the Black Hills, is in Cheyenne, or I'll scalp you alive and hang you to a telegraph pole. You hear me, and don't you forget it. CALAMITY JANE (Spring, p. 214)."

Not a pretty woman, Calamity's rough looks let her pass as a mule skinner, bull whacker and freight driver without anyone suspecting that she was a she. As a matter of fact, she was often mistaken for a man—she smoked and chewed like one, she drank like one, she smelled like one, she gambled like one, and she worked like one. In most of the towns of the West that she frequented, she was treated like a man. (And don't forget, she was probably being paid a man's wages, something few women could claim in the 1800s.)

But in Martha Jane Cannary's lonely mind, a mind more familiar with the rear ends of teams of mules than a romantic encounter in the front parlor, she claimed she married Hickok. She said they'd married in September 1871. They had a child, Calamity claimed. The child, a daughter, was born on September 25, 1873. This "daughter" came forth with the "proof" of marriage some forty years after Calamity died.

In a diary, purportedly kept by Calamity Jane, she wrote under an entry for September 1880: "I met James Butler Hickok Wild Bill in 1870 near Abilene Kansas—I heard a bunch of outlaws planning to kill him I couldn't get to where my horse was so I crawled on my hands and knees through the brush past the outlaws for over a mile and reached the old shack where he was staying that night I told him and he hid me back of the door while he shot it out with them Bill killed them all while on the trip to Abilene we met Rev Sipes and Rev Warren and we were married (McCormick, p. 8)."

Was it so? Calamity Jane's proof is in the diary. In this diary, she also met Jesse James. This meeting, which certainly would have been a momentous occasion, was recorded in the diary. Of course, it occurred seven years after young Bob Ford put a bullet in Jesse's brain.

And what did Calamity Jane get out of all of this? In 1903, on August 1, she died of pneumonia in a Terry, Montana, hotel. She had asked to be buried in Deadwood next to Hickok. Her wish was granted and she joined Hickok on Mount Moriah overlooking Deadwood. (Some claim that Deadwood had a special place in its heart for Calamity since she had nursed many of its residents back to health during a devastating smallpox epidemic. They at least thought enough of her to enter her death date as August 2— the same day Hickok was killed, rather than the actual date of death, August 1.)

Born in Missouri, Calamity was orphaned in Montana while in her teens. Without formal education, she began carving a crude life for herself in a world that was primarily a man's world. Her many adventures, brushes with death, and meetings with famous people often seemed to be created in her mind. She was never known to permit the truth to stand in the way of a wholesome lie.

Hickok's friend at Abilene, Charles Gross, remembering from a distance of fifty-some years, told J.B. Edwards, "The many talks I had with Bill I do not now recall any remark, or reference to any Woman other than those he made to the One he lived with in the Small house & he did not Ever show before me any Especial affection for her—What he called her I do not recall but *I do Know he was on Guard Even against her* I was there alone with the two Many times but I was Very careful never to go unless I knew Bill was Home & always there was good reason for my going. Having to go Early one morning Bill was still in Bed & when I went to the door and the woman came to let me in she saw through the window who I was.—she was only just up & was still in night dress Bill said 'let him in; you don't give a Dam for Gross seeing you' but she did and showed it in looks (Gross letter to Edwards, June 15, 1925)."

But evidently, James Butler Hickok did meet his wife in Abilene. It was during the summer that he was the city marshal and during July that Hickok's future wife came to town. Her name was Agnes Mersman Thatcher Lake.

Mrs. Lake's "Hippo-Olympiad and Mammoth Circus" came to town on the Kansas Pacific Railroad. Not much is known about the circus. It appeared on July 13, 1871, and the Abilene *Chronicle* of August 3 reported, "The attendance was large at each performance."

To be sure, it was an exciting time for the people of Abilene. Respectable, honest entertainment was always eagerly sought by folks living west of Kansas City. The circus, in particular, was always welcomed.

Circuses, not new to the West, had first come to the present continental United States from Mexico. European troupes were brought over and invariably worked their way north into Mexican Texas and California. Included in some of these circuses and in the later circuses that invaded Kansas and Nebraska, were animals,

The Killing Time

clowns, and all kinds of stunts, including tightrope walkers and high-wire artists. The entire troupe paraded from the railroad track through Abilene to the fair grounds outside the city.

Once there, they set up the tent—with anxious youngsters milling about, taking in the sights and sounds of circus excitement. And then it was time for the show to go on.

In the center ring, the elephant show or horses being ridden by riders standing on their backs, were featured acts. All of this, of course, was to the music of a brass band. There were side shows—a strong man, the tattooed lady, a magician.

So it was there at the "Hippo-Olympiad and Mammoth Circus" in the cooling shade of the big top that Marshal Hickok may have met the owner of the circus, Mrs. Agnes Lake for the first time. At the time, Mrs. Lake was about forty-five years old. A native of Doehme, Alsace, young Agnes Mersman emigrated to Cincinnati, Ohio, with her parents when she was a girl. By the mid-1840s, Agnes was interested in the circus, so interested that she eloped with a circus clown named William Lake Thatcher. (Later, the clown dropped the last name, opting for the shorter name of Lake.)

The Ohio and Mississippi rivers became the home of the Lakes as they worked on a floating circus known as the Spalding and Rogers Circus. For fifteen to twenty years they had a circus life together. She worked as an equestrian, riding the loping horses in the center ring, balancing on their bare backs in front of the cheering crowds. In addition, Mrs. Lake had a high-wire act that thrilled audiences as she teetered high above the sawdust floor of the center ring.

Then, in the 1860s, Agnes Mersman Lake was widowed when William Lake was shot to death by a circus employee. The widowed Mrs. Lake continued to operate the circus, the capacity in which she was working when she first met Hickok.

Between July 1871 and March 1876, Hickok and Mrs. Lake carried on a correspondence which led the two of them to Cheyenne, Wyoming. There, on March 5, 1876, S.L. Moyer and his wife witnessed the Methodist wedding of James Butler Hickok and Agnes Mersman Lake Thatcher (Rosa, *They Called Him Wild Bill*, p. 234-238).

The Cheyenne *Daily Leader* carried the story two days later: "MARRIED.—By the Rev. W.F. Warren, March 5th, 1876, at the residence of S.L. Moyer, Cheyenne, Wyoming territory, Mrs. Agnes Lake Thatcher of Cincinnati, Ohio to James Butler Hickok, Wild Bill, of this city (Cheyenne *Daily Leader*, Mar. 7, 1876)."

As always, Hickok was news. And this time it was not a report of his death that lit up the newspapers in the East and West. The Cheyenne *Daily Sun*, of March 8, 1876, noted: "'Wild Bill,' of Western fame, has conquered numerous Indians, outlaws, bears and buffaloes, but a charming widow has stolen the magic wand. The scepter has departed, and he is as meek and gentle as a lamb. In other words, he has shuffled off the coils of bachelorhood."

The Omaha *Daily Bee*, of March 31, 1876, noted: "Hickok has always been considered wild and woolly and hard to curry but the proprietress of the best circus on the continent wanted a husband of renown so she laid siege to the not over susceptible heart of the man who has killed his dozens of both whites and Indians."

The Hickoks grabbed an eastbound train and returned to her hometown of Cincinnati for a two-week honeymoon. Hickok then left her with relatives while he returned to St. Louis to put into operation his plan to organize a band of miners to take to the Black Hills. When he had made enough money, he would send for his wife and they would live in the West. Strangely, it was the same deal that young James Butler Hickok had made with his mother, brothers and sisters twenty years earlier. This time, instead of striking it rich in Kansas and sending for them, Dakota was the place where Hickok would go to get rich.

The Black Hills, land that clearly belonged to various American Indian tribes, was desecrated in the summer of 1874 by Lt. Colonel George Armstrong Custer, ten companies of the 7th U.S. Cavalry, two companies of infantry, photographer W.H. Illingsworth, Yale ethnologist George Bird Grinnel, two experienced gold miners, and President U.S. Grant's son Frederick Dent Grant. With this expedition came over one hundred wagons and ambulances, a herd of beef cattle, three Gatling guns and a three-inch cannon.

By the Treaty of 1868, this expedition was illegal. The treaty stated: "No white person or persons shall be permitted to settle upon or occupy any portion of the territory, or without the consent of the Indians to pass through the same."

But there was gold involved. The "yellow metal that makes the white man crazy" was all the excuse anyone in Washington needed. Then Custer sent one of his scouts, Charley Reynolds, to bring the message to the world. Within days and weeks, all of the United States read accounts of great quantities of gold to be had in the Black Hills. Would-be miners and millionaires prepared for an assault on the sacred hills and by 1876, the various tribes of native people were no longer much of a concern. It became easier for the U.S. Army to deal with the irate Indians than the gold-mad whites from the East.

Meanwhile, in the spring of 1876, in St. Louis, Hickok abandoned his idea of organizing a band of miners to go into the Black Hills. He opted instead to go it alone to Cheyenne. Then he'd continue on to Deadwood, Dakota Territory, in the Black Hills.

The Black Hills were beautiful at that time of the year. Unlike the blistering barrenness of the plains, the hills were a refuge from the dry heat that surrounded them. It was an oasis in the middle of a semi-arid region. Raised to an elevation of about 4,000 feet out of the earth's crust geological eras ago, the Black Hills offered shady canyons, spectacular rock formations, clear cool streams, and the smell of tall, pine forests.

To the American Indian tribes in the area, the hills were sacred, a holy place. The Great Spirit had given them the hills as a haven, a place to return to when the people were threatened by severe weather or shortage of food and water. Even the deer, antelope, and buffalo used the hills in that way.

In late June, Hickok and his friends, California Joe (Moses Embree Milner) and Colorado Charley (Charles H. Utter), left Cheyenne for Deadwood and the Black Hills. They arrived at Deadwood Gulch at the north end of the 120-mile-long chain of hills about the end of the first week of July. At that time, Hickok told his companions, "Boys, I have a hunch that I am in my last camp and will never leave this gulch alive."

On the night of August 1, he said about the same thing to Tom Dosier, another acquaintance. Hickok told Dosier, "Tom, I have a presentiment that my time is up and that I am going to be killed (Connelley, p. 202)."

And history claims that Hickok posted a letter to his wife on the first day of August:

Dead Wood Black Hills Dakota
August 1st 1876

Agnes Darling,

If such should be we never meet again, while firing my last shot I will gently breathe the name of my wife—Agnes—and with wishes even for my enemies I will take the plunge and try to swim to the other shore.

J.B. Hickok
Wild Bill (Buel, p. 210-211)

The next day, August 2, a Wednesday, Hickok walked down the street to Carl Mann and Jerry Lewis' Number Ten saloon. It was about 3 P.M. when he entered the plain, rough-board saloon. His eyes adjusted to the light and he noticed Carl Mann and several others playing poker at the rear, about twenty feet away, near the back door of the saloon.

The men invited him to take a seat and play. Charlie Rich sat on a stool, his back to the wall. Across from William Rodney Massie, a Missouri River steamboat captain, was an empty chair. Hickok asked about Rich's seat. He wondered aloud if Rich would mind trading with him. Hickok wanted the seat where his back was to the wall. He was vulnerable from the backside, the blind side. It was the one area that his eyes could not detect trouble at a distance safe for pistol fire. He'd have to be careful of that.

Not only Rich laughed at him for wanting the seat with the wall to his back, but so did Massie and Mann. Hickok said nothing. But then, while the cards were being shuffled in preparation for the game to start, Hickok asked Rich again. Could he sit there, have the stool on the wall? Again all three players teased Hickok.

The back door stood open letting the air pass through the saloon, cooling the room. Hickok couldn't get the problem out of his mind. His back was wide open. The door stood open, his back to it.

Hickok was losing. He couldn't concentrate with his back exposed like this. Remember. Captain Massie was winning, getting back some of the money he'd lost the previous evening to Hickok.

The game had gone on for about an hour when the front door opened and a slight man entered. One of his eyes was crossed and his nose was smashed against his face. He was a hard-looking man in a mining town full of hard-looking men.

At the crude bar, the ugly man ordered whiskey, then nervously drank it. All the time, his good eye was checking over the room. Counting Hickok and the bartender, the hard man saw seven men. And then he sized up Hickok's location.

While he stared at Hickok, Hickok called to the bartender, Harry Young, and asked that he bring over $15 in pocket checks. In just an hour, Hickok had lost all the money he had with him. With the checks, the game continued, and the conversation between Hickok and Massie grew irritated.

Just minutes later, the man at the bar stepped toward the end of it, then started toward the back door. When within three or four feet of the door, he turned and produced a pistol.

Hickok and Massie were arguing. Hickok said, "The old duffer—he broke me on the hand."

It was ten minutes past four. The man behind Hickok had a Navy-sized revolver in his hand. He held it "from one foot to eighteen inches" from the back of Hickok's head. He jerked the trigger and in the midst of the roar of the pistol, he cried out, "Damn you! Take that!"

The bullet traveled a fatal path, entering the base of the brain and out through the upper and lower jaw bones. The bullet crossed the table and lodged in Capt. Massie's wrist.

The bartender and another man moved toward Hickok, but the shooter swung in their direction and yelled, "Come on ye sons of bitches!" He snapped the pistol twice. It did not discharge.

There was a general stampede for the front door while the killer ran out the back door. Carl Mann, still at the table, recalled what happened to Hickok. Mann said, "It kind of knocked Bill's head forward and then he fell gradually back."

By Hickok's left hand on the floor, there was his last poker hand—the eight of Clubs, the eight of Spades, the ace of Spades, the ace of Clubs, and a Diamond face card. Aces and Eights, the Dead Man's Hand.

The murderer was captured a short time later in Jacob Shroudy's butcher shop. For a time, a group of men debated whether to hang him on the spot. But then a rider from Crook City said Indians were attacking there and every man who had a horse or could rent one decided that was more exciting. Jack McCall, the killer, was held captive, twenty-five men forming a guard.

Ellis T. (Doc) Pierce, local medical man, barber and undertaker, prepared Hickok's body. The head wound had drained the blood from the body. Hickok made a handsome corpse, his face and hands marble white, the black broadcloth suit and white linen shirt, the parted hair with ringlets over the shoulders framing the face.

Hickok's friends found a rough pine coffin, covered it with black cloth and lined it with white. Carefully, they eased Hickok into it. They placed his old rifle in the coffin with their friend.

McCall's trial took place the next day, August 3. He told the court, "Wild Bill killed my brother, and I killed him. Wild Bill threatened to kill me if I ever crossed his path. I am not sorry for what I have done. If I had to, I would do the same thing over again."

Someone went to the printers and had signs made up to be posted in Deadwood:

Died, in Deadwood, Black Hills August 2, 1876, from the effect of a pistol shot, J.B. Hickok, (Wild Bill) formerly of Cheyenne, Wyoming. Funeral Services will be held at Charlie Utter's camp, on Thursday afternoon. August 3, 1876, at 3 o'clock. All are respectfully invited to attend (Connelley, p. 206).

The services went as expected. Bill Hillman, John Oyster, Charlie Rich, Jerry Lewis, Charlie Young, and Tom Dosier were pallbearers. Hickok was buried at Ingleside.

Three years later, the body was moved to Mount Moriah Cemetery. Hickok started out with a wooden headboard, but souvenir hunters made short work of that, whittling pieces off it. In 1891, a New York sculptor, J.B. Riordan, set a stone bust on a rock base. By 1902, that was in bad shape and a life-sized, sandstone monument of Hickok was sculpted by Alvin Smith. It went up in 1903. A wire fence did little to deter new souvenir hunters. By 1925, even the fence was gone. The fifth marker, a stone one, now heads the grave (Rosa, *They Called Him Wild Bill*, p. 305-306).

Meanwhile, back in town, the trial of Jack McCall went on. At 7:30 that night, Judge W.S. Kuykendall received the verdict of the jury: "We, the jurors, find the prisoner, Mr. John McCall, not guilty."

McCall was arrested and brought to trial again. The first trial was held on land owned by the Indians, that as a result of the Treaty of 1868. Whites were not in the Black Hills legally. The new trial commenced on December 4, 1876, at Yankton, Dakota Territory. Two days later, the jury returned a verdict of "Guilty." McCall was hanged at 10:15 A.M. on March 1, 1877 (Connelley, p. 213).

There was still talk about Hickok's anticipation of death, his presentiments. *The Pioneer-Press and Tribune*, St. Paul, Minnesota,

September 7, 1876, carried a story that it had picked up about Hickok's premonition of death from the August 26, 1876, *Cheyenne Leader*.

Wild Bill's Presentiment

A week before Wild Bill's death he was heard to remark to a friend: "I feel that my days are numbered; my sun is sinking fast; I know I shall be killed here; something tells me I shall never leave these hills alive. But I don't know who it is or why he is going to do it. I have killed many men in my day, but I never killed a man but it was kill or get killed with me. But I have two trusty friends—the one is my six-shooter and the other is California Joe." Could California Joe have arrived in time no doubt McCall would have been hanged, but he was down at Crook City looking for Indians. On Friday, the morning after the shooting, Joe came to Deadwood, and after hearing all the particulars of the killing of Wild Bill, walked down to McCall's cabin and calling him out asked him if he didn't think the air about there was rather light for him. McCall's cheeks blanched, and he feebly answered that he thought it was. "Well, I guess you had better take a walk, then," said Joe, and seating himself on the side of the hill he watched the retreating figure out of sight. And this is the second murderer who has been permitted to leave the Black Hills without being held in any way for the crime."

The August 17, 1876, *Ellis County Star* reported:

We learn from recent dispatches that Mr. J.B. Hickok, (Wild Bill), well known to the older citizens of Hays City, was shot in the head and instantly killed, by a man named Bill Sutherland, while playing cards in a saloon in Deadwood Gulch, Wyoming.

Even in death, the newspapers couldn't get it right.

Epilogue

It was a beautiful day. The May 31, 1904, *Kansas City Journal* called it "perfect, with clear blue sky and balmy air." The procession marched solemnly north through Abilene, headed for the cemetery north of town.

The children were giddy with the excitement of the day. There was red, white and blue bunting everywhere. The American flag fluttered peacefully over many of the large houses on the broad, shady street. It was Memorial Day, May 30, 1904.

The procession, now a mile long, continued on, the Abilene Military Band leading the way. It was a festive day, one that everyone would remember. For it was today that Abilene would pay its respects to a man who helped bring Abilene from lawlessness to civilization. His name: Thomas James Smith.

Some of the older adults in the procession remembered how it was when Tom Smith was the marshal of Abilene. They remembered the Texans, the cattle, the smell, the great clouds of dust by the stockyards. And melancholy slipped over them, remembering their youth and wondering where all the years had gone.

They had been young and full of energy, their lives ahead of them. That was over thirty years ago. Marshal Smith had missed all that. Dead all those years. But what had he missed?

Abilene had grown. Civilization had marched across these Kansas plains; marching, marching, marching. The times, they had changed between 1870 and 1904.

People from all over Dickinson County and Kansas were in Abilene to join in the special ceremony. It was a huge crowd, "One of the largest crowds ever in this city," according to the *Journal* (The *Kansas City Journal*, May 31, 1904). There was to be a new interment and placing of the monument for Tom Smith.

For all those who had heard the story of Bear River Tom Smith, this was a chance to be a part of history. The Abilene Military Band, Grand Army of the Republic, Abilene Fire Department, speakers of the day, citizens' committee in carriages, mayor and city councilmen, fraternal organizations, and general public made up the lengthy procession.

The Grand Army of the Republic began the ceremonies. Men held their hats over their hearts or saluted. Women and children stood at attention. Abilene's Military Band played the "Star Spangled Banner." The G.A.R. Post Commander spoke and the Invocation was given. James R. Gower recited the Gettysburg Address.

At the close of the ceremony, the crowd gathered at Smith's new gravesite, a 4,480-pound, red granite boulder shipped in from Granite Mountain in Oklahoma now marking the new grave. J.B. Edwards had purchased the stone and shipped it. He and others defrayed some of the expenses by selling photos of Smith and, some say, Hickok.

W.H. Eicholtz, who had buried Smith, prepared a new metal casket. A bronze plaque attached to the granite boulder told Smith's story:

THOMAS J. SMITH
Marshal of Abilene, 1870.
Died, a Martyr to Duty, Nov. 2, 1870.
A Fearless Hero of Frontier Days
Who in Cowboy Chaos
Established the Supremacy of Law
(Abilene *Daily Chronicle*, May 31, 1904).

A leading attorney, W.S. Stambaugh, addressed the crowd and turned over the new monument and lot in the cemetery to the city. Abilene's Mayor S.R. Cowan accepted the monument and then spoke to those assembled. He said, in part, of Smith, "He never feared to meet his enemies face to face; their number and the strength of their position never disturbed him. He had confidence in himself and in his cause. He hazarded everything in defense of what he thought was right, and was bent on doing his duty or finding his grave in the attempt. Never before or since have we had an officer of the law more valuable or more efficient.... Abilene is a clean town, a law-abiding town, largely because of what this man accomplished ("Two City Marshals," p. 527)."

The crowd moved back to town where a public meeting was held at the Seelye Theater at 2 P.M. Flags and bunting adorned the stage. "About 100 old soldiers" sat on the stage and "scores of old settlers" shuffled down the aisles to find a seat. There was a double quartet and John Johntz presided.

Former Mayor T.C. Henry spoke first, reminding all of their history. He began, "Lips far more eloquent than mine have many times before told the story of the struggle, out of which has grown a political entity whose grandeur is unrivaled in all the history of nations."

Continuing, Henry pointed out, "It is our privilege this day, and here, to pay double honor—honor to those who preserved the institutions of liberty planted by our forefathers—and honor to one whose unsurpassed bravery subdued disorder, conquered lawlessness and made clear the way for the blessings of peace and prosperity, whose fruitions you people of Abilene, the beautiful, and Dickinson, the grand, enjoy."

Smith and Hickok. They were preservers of the institutions of liberty. They subdued disorder. But they were different. They gave Abilene different answers to the same questions. Hickok left a different impression than Smith.

Put simply, a mother in Abilene in 1870 wanted her son to grow up like Tom Smith—handsome, brave, caring, sober.

In 1871, when an Abilene mother wanted to regain control of her rambunctious children, she didn't threaten them with the promise of a visit from the bogeyman. That was not necessary. Real fear spread through the children when their mother invoked the name, "Wild Bill."

He was gentle in manners, low-toned in speech, deferential in the presence of official superiors, and brave beyond question. He serves first place in the gallery of frontier marshals.

Mayor T.C. Henry
Abilene, Kansas

That was Mayor Henry's opinion of Thomas James Smith. But where did that leave James Butler Hickok. J.B. Edwards, in an interview, said of Hickok:

His bravery has been described by old-timers in Abilene as cruder than Tom Smith's. Many believed that Wild Bill without the guns would have been tame.

Kansas City Star,
November 15, 1925

Edwards, in 1896, delved into Hickok's psyche even more. Edwards explained, "His very notoriety seemed to cause many men to be jealous of him." Edwards went on to describe Hickok as "over-bearing when from any cause he became cross at anyone."

Certainly, 1871 was a bad year to hire on as city marshal in Abilene, Kansas. Smith had laid down the law the previous year. Stuart Henry, Mayor Henry's brother, wrote, "Smith's *regime* of disarmament the summer before, his almost perfect control, made Bill's line of duties far easier than his predecessor's. Smith...paved a smooth way or showed that the back of wild Texans domination could at any time be broken."

According to Henry, "Wild Bill needed merely to continue Smith's achieved program, which he did in the main or after a fashion. He prevented murders and destruction of property through the dread of his twin pistols, and for this he deserved and received credit, especially since the Cattle Trade was larger (Henry, S., p. 273-274)."

Epilogue

As a lawman, Hickok was not trained as Smith had been. Hickok had a different style. Smith patrolled the streets; Hickok seldom did. While Smith rode his horse down the center of the streets, with just his presence preventing the breaking of Abilene's laws, Hickok preferred the Alamo Saloon and a friendly game of poker—with his back to the wall.

Stuart Henry wrote of Smith, "He, unlike Bill, gave his whole time and his thought to his duties without assistants." On the other hand, Hickok, in Henry's estimation, "ruled by his pistols alone."

Mayor Henry noted another difference in Smith and Hickok. He realized that he'd never seen Tom Smith's pistols when he was on duty. On the contrary, "Wild Bill...never forgot that he was armed and could shoot first." Henry added that Hickok's "bearing and bravery were of a far lower type (Henry, S., p. 285)."

But Hickok came to Abilene with a reputation. It was a reputation that said he, Wild Bill, had killed more white, civilian men than any other gunman. He was a two-pistol shooter, which made him different from most of the gunfighters. He carried two pistols, butts forward, and could draw them from his belt or sash and shoot with both hands.

Hickok was perceived as being a fair man, a gunfighter who was honorable. He was a man who shot and killed men only when they needed it, were armed, and had a fair chance to defend themselves. It was an honorable match, one built around the dueling codes of the gentlemen of the Old World. That is what Abilene thought it was getting in the spring of 1871.

As it turned out, they got law enforcement of a sort. The only men he killed on this job were a Texas saloonkeeper, who got drunk and disturbed the peace while shooting at a dog, and a special policeman who came running to the sound of gunfire and ran directly into the history books—with the help of Wild Bill's deadly, blazing guns.

Such was life on the American frontier; such was life for the lawmen who helped bring Abilene from lawlessness to civilization.

Bibliography

Books, Articles & Unpublished Materials:

"An Early Day Hero," *Kansas City Journal*, May 31, 1904.

"Brought Order to Abilene," Kansas City (MO) *Star*, September 29, 1899.

Brown, Dee Alexander. *The Gentle Tamers: Women of the Old West*. Lincoln, NE: University of Nebraska Press, 1970.

———. *Hear That Lonesome Whistle Blow*. NY: Holt, Rinehart and Winston, 1977.

———. *Wondrous Times on the Frontier*. Little Rock, AR: August House Publishers, Inc., 1991.

Brown, Dee and Martin F. Schmitt. *Trail Driving Days*. NY: Bonanza Books, 1952.

Bryan, Jerry. "An Illinois Gold Hunter in the Black Hills," (Diary, March 13-August 20, 1876). Pamphlet Series No. 2, Illinois State Historical Society, Springfield, IL, 1960.

Buel, J.W. *Heroes of the Plains*. St. Louis, MO: Sun Publishing Co., 1882.

Butler, Anne M. *Daughters of Joy, Sisters of Misery: Prostitutes in the American West 1865-90*. Urbana and Chicago, IL: University of Illinois Press, 1987.

"City Council Minute Book," Records of the City of Abilene.

Connelley, William E. *Wild Bill and His Era*. NY: The Press of Pioneers, 1933.

Cushman, George L., "Abilene, First of the Kansas Cow Towns," The Kansas Historical Quarterly, vol. ix, no. 3. (August 1940)

Bibliography

Custer, Elizabeth Bacon. *Following the Guidon*. Norman, OK: University of Oklahoma Press, 1962.

Custer, George Armstrong. *My Life on the Plains*. Norman, OK: University of Oklahoma Press, 1967.

Dary, David. *Cowboy Culture: A Saga of Five Centuries*. NY: Alfred A. Knopf, 1981.

———. "Thomas James Smith: Abilene Marshal," Kanhistique. January 1977.

———. *True Tales of the Old-Time Plains*. NY: Crown Publishers, Inc., 1979.

Davidson, Sherwood. "Early Recollections of Sherwood Davidson." (Unpublished manuscript.)

DeArment, Robert K. *Knights of the Green Cloth: The Saga of the Frontier Gamblers*. Norman, OK: University of Oklahoma Press, 1982.

Drago, Harry Sinclair. *Wild, Woolly & Wicked*. NY: Clarkson N. Potter, Inc., 1960.

Duffield, George C. "Driving Cattle from Texas to Iowa," Annals of Iowa. Series 3, vol. 14 (April 1924).

Dunham, Jim. "James Butler Hickok: Prince of Pistoleers," *Guns and the Gunfighters*. NY: Bonanza Books, 1982.

Dykstra, Robert R. *The Cattle Towns*. Lincoln, NE: University of Nebraska Press, 1983.

Edwards, J.B. *Early Days in Abilene*. Abilene, KS, 1940.

Forbis, William H. *The Cowboys*. NY: Time-Life Books, 1973.

Fetterolf, Jerry. "Abilene Reveres Memory of Greatest Marshal," Topeka (KS) *Capital-Journal*, January 25, 1959.

Gross, Charles, to J.B. Edwards, August 23, 1922; June 15, 1925. "J.B. Edwards Collection," (Manuscripts) Kansas State Historical Society, Topeka.

Hansen, George W. "True Story of Will Bill—McCanles Affray in Jefferson County, Nebraska, July 12, 1861," *Nebraska History Magazine*, vol. x, no. 2 (April-June, 1927).

Hardin, J.W. *The Life of John Wesley Hardin As Written by Himself*. Norman, OK: University of Oklahoma Press, 1961.

Harper's New Weekly Magazine, vol. xxxiv, February 1867.

Heisler, E.F. and D.M. Smith. Atlas Map of Johnson County, Kansas. Wyandotte, 1874.

Henry, Stuart. *Conquering Our Great American Plains*. NY: E.P.Dutton & Co., 1930.

Jameson, Henry B. *Heroes by the Dozen: Abilene—Cattle Days to President Ike*. Abilene, KS: Shadinger-Wilson Printers, Inc., 1961.

Kane, Richard A. (Letter to the Editor), "The D.A. vs. S.A. Controversy," *Outdoor Life*, vol. xvii, no. 6 (June 1906).

Little, Theophilus, "Early Days of Abilene and Dickinson County," in Roenigk, Adolph ed. *Pioneer History of Kansas*. Lincoln, KS, 1933.

Long, Mrs. L.H. "Some Incidents in the Death of Tom Smith," (As told by Mrs. Long to H.L. Humphrey) (Unpublished manuscript.) December 26, 1931.

McCaleb, J.L. "My First Five-Dollar Bill," *The Trail Drivers of Texas*. vol. i. J. Marvin Hunter, ed. NY: Argosy-Antiquarian Ltd., 1963.

McCormick, Jean Hickok. *Calamity Jane's Diary and Letters*, 1951.

McCoy, Joseph G. *Cattle Trade of the West and Southwest*. Kansas City, MO: Ramsey, Millett & Hudson, 1874. (Reprint. Ann Arbor, MI: University Microfilms, Inc., 1966.)

Miller, Nyle H. and Joseph W. Snell. *Great Gunfighters of the Kansas Cowtowns, 1867-1886*. Lincoln, NE: University of Nebraska Press, 1967.

Monaghan, James. *The Great Rascal: The Life and Adventures of Ned Buntline*. NY: Bonanza Books, 1951.

Moore, Howard. "No Flowers on Grave of Tom Smith, Pioneer Hero," Abilene (KS) *Reflector-Chronicle*, May 31, 1956.

Nichols, Walter D. "The Death of Tom Smith," (As told to H.L. Humphrey.) (Unpublished manuscript.) December 26, 1931.

Oliva, Leo E. *Fort Hays, Frontier Army Post: 1865-89*. Topeka, NE: Kansas State Historical Society, 1980.

Parsons, Chuck. "Phil Coe: Professional Gambler from Texas," *Quarterly of the National Association and Center for Outlaw and Lawman History*. vol. iv, no. 1, Summer, 1978. pp. 14-20.

Patterson, Richard. *Historical Atlas of the Outlaw West*. Boulder, CO: Johnson Books, 1985.

Bibliography

Richardson, Leander P. "A Trip to the Black Hills," *Scribner's Monthly*, vol. xiii (February 1877).

Robinson, A.W. Detroit (KS) *Western News*, April 11, 1870.

Roenigk, Adolph, ed. *Pioneer History of Kansas*. Lincoln, KS, 1933.

Rosa, Joseph G. *They Called Him Wild Bill: The Life and Adventures of James Butler Hickok*. Norman: University of Oklahoma Press, 1982.

———. "Wild Bill Hickok—Peacemaker," Reprinted from Volume I of *The Prairie Scout, Kansas Corral of Westerners* (no date).

Rybolt, Robert. "Requiem for John Kile," *Old West*, vol. 30, no. 3, Spring 1995 (pp. 28-32.)

Spring, Agnes Wright. *The Cheyenne and Black Hills Stage and Express Route*. Lincoln, NE: University of Nebraska Press, 1948.

Stanley, Henry M. *My Early Travels and Adventures in America and Asia*. London, 1895.

Stratton, Joanna L. *Pioneer Women: Voices from the Kansas Frontier*. NY: Simon & Shuster, 1981.

Streeter, Floyd Benjamin. *Prairie Trails & Cow Towns: The Opening of the Old West*. NY: The Devin Adair Company, 1963. (1936)

———. *The Kaw*. NY: Farrar & Rhinehart, Inc., 1941.

"Two City Marshals," *Collections*, Kansas State Historical Society, Vol. IX, pp. 526-532.

Underwood, Larry D. *The Custer Fight and Other Tales of the Old West*. Lincoln, NE: Media Publishing, 1989.

———. *Guns, Gold and Glory*. Lincoln, NE: Media Publishing, 1992.

———. *Love and Glory: Women of the Old West*. Lincoln, NE: Dageforde Publishing, Inc. 1991.

Van Patten, M.D., Edwin H. "A Brief History of David McCoy and Family," *Journal of the Illinois State Historical Society*. vol. 14 (1921)

Verckler, Stewart P. *Cowtown—Abilene: The Story of Abilene, Kansas 1867-1875*. NY: Carleton Press, 1961.

Walton, W.M. *Life and Adventures of Ben Thompson The Famous Texan*. Austin, TX: Steck and Company, 1956.

Wellman, Paul I. *The Trampling Herd*. NY: Carrick & Edwards, Inc., 1939.

Newspapers:

Abilene (KS)*Chronicle*.

Abilene (KS) *Daily Chronicle*.

Abilene (KS) *Reflector-Chronicle*.

Austin (TX) *Daily Democratic Statesman*.

Brenham (TX) *Banner*.

Chapman (KS) *Advertiser*, May 22, 1969.

Cheyenne (WY) *Daily Leader*, March 7, 1876.

Cheyenne (WY) *Daily Sun*, March 8, 1876.

Clyde (KS) *Republican Valley Empire*.

The *Dickinson County Chronicle*

Detroit (KS) *Western News*.

Ellis County (KS) *Star*.

Junction City (KS) *Union*.

Kansas City (MO) *Star*.

The *Kansas City Journal*.

Leavenworth (KS) *Commonwealth*.

Leavenworth (KS) *Daily Conservative*.

Leavenworth (KS) *Daily Times*.

Leavenworth (KS) *Times and Conservative*.

Omaha (NE) *Daily Bee*, March 31, 1876.

Rochester (NY) *Democrat and Chronicle*.

St. Paul (MN) *The Pioneer-Press and Tribune*.

Salina (KS) *Saline County Journal*.

Springfield (MO) *Weekly Patriot*.

Topeka (KS) *Capital*.

Topeka (KS) *Capital-Journal*.

Topeka (KS) *Kansas Daily Commonwealth*.

Wichita (KS) *Tribune*.

Endnotes

1   There were also others involved in the project, causing Dykstra to point out that McCoy's involvement was not singular. See Dykstra, p. 20-21. Dykstra implies that Samuel N. Hitt was also involved. See Dykstra, p. 163.

2   Shane was the agent for about 200,000 acres opened to settlement by the Kansas Pacific Railroad. Shane kept the books while Henry sold the land.

3   The Smith-Henry conversation was reconstructed by T.C. Henry.

4   These accounts were drawn heavily from T.C. Henry's recollections when he spoke in Abilene in 1904. This is included in: T.C. Henry's address at the May 30, 1904 memorial services for Tom Smith ("Two City Marshals," p. 526-532).

5   A recent search of census and court records in Kansas and reported in David Dary's *Cowboy Culture: A Saga of Five Centuries* reveals that the Kansas cow town prostitutes were 17, 18, or 19 years old. They were mainly white and usually unmarried. Beyond that, the research showed, "The girls were short or tall, fat or thin, pretty or homely. They came from good families and bad. Prostitution was a melting pot where the only general criterion was possession of a female body." (Dary, p. 218).

6   At some time during 1870, Abilene presented Smith with a brace of nickel-plated revolvers. (Henry, S., p. 208).

7   Davidson, in his 1932 recollections, did not indicate if he went along to protect McConnell or not. He does not say whether or how Miles may have returned home.

8   Senator Wilson later became vice-president of the United States during President U.S. Grant's second term.

9   Hickok once mentioned this fight to Charles Gross: "I never shot a man with my left hand Except the time with some drunken Soldiers had me down on the floor & were trampling me & then I used both hands." Gross, Charles, to J.B. Edwards, June 15, 1925. "J.B. Edwards Collection," (Manuscripts) Kansas State Historical Society, Topeka.

10   Besides Rosa, p. 156-60, there are others. They include: Rybolt, Robert. "Requiem for John Kile," *Old West*. Vol. 30, No. 3, Spring 1995. (pp. 28-32.) Also see: Topeka (KS) *Kansas Daily Commonwealth*, July 22, 1870. Junction City (KS) July 23, 1870. Clyde (KS) *Republican Valley Empire*, August 2, 1870.

11   Joseph G. Rosa, a Hickok biographer, related in *They Called Him Wild Bill: The Life and Adventures of James Butler Hickok*, that he had some doubt about McCanles not being armed. But even Rosa admits, "The question whether or not the McCanles party were armed can never be settled for sure."

12   Kane claimed this occurred outside Milwaukee, Wisconsin. Joseph G. Rosa, in his investigation of the affair in 1960, found that Hickok did not play in Milwaukee with Cody and Omohundro.

13   Hickok, by the way, married only once. At the time, he was thirty-eight. His wife, the widow Agnes Lake Thatcher, was almost fifty.

14   Here the judge probably referred to the eyewitnesses who all testified that they had seen the incident. They added that Tutt fired his weapon first. The revolver, retrieved from the area of the body, was prominently displayed in court.

15   Nichols eventually moved to Cincinnati, helped to found the School of Design, and, with the help of Reuben R. Springer, established the Cincinnati College of Music during 1879.

Nichols served as the president of that college until his death in 1885.

16   And an 1871 census reported that Abilene had 32 places selling alcoholic beverages—not all saloons, 64 gambling tables and 130 known gamblers.)

17   Leavenworth (KS) *Commonwealth*, May 11, 1871. (A $200 fee was finally passed into law—and again the political fur flew when Eicholtz and Brinkman resigned. See "City Council Minute Book," Records of the City of Abilene. May 31, 1871. A reconstituted council eventually reduced the amount to $100. Politics is politics.

18   Carson and McDonald had a dispute which led to them being reprimanded by council President, J.A. Gauthie. Just over a month later, there was a controversy between Marshal Hickok and McDonald. This controversy revolved around $20.

19   Norton and Carson were on the job only for a couple of months. Later on, the two had a shootout which left Norton wounded and Carson under arrest.

20   Coe was also in violation of Kansas law. For some time, Kansas had a state law against carrying a weapon—"a pistol, bowie knife, dirk or other deadly weapon"— if vagrant, intoxicated or a former Confederate soldier. (Dykstra, p. 121).

21   Stuart Henry wrote of Hickok, "His interest and time were divided by gambling." As a result of that, according to Henry, "He didn't remain strict about the ordinance, and witnessed with no great dissatisfaction the growing habit of men with pistols at hand when they wanted to shoot."

22   Some modern historians suggest that these were not Englishmen being guided by Cody and company, but rather a group headed by a Chicago saloon keeper.

Index

Index

Index

Index

Dageforde Publishing, Inc.

Visit us on our web site: www.dageforde.com
email: info@dageforde.com

Abilene Lawmen: The Smith-Hickok Years Larry D. Underwood, ISBN 1-886225-40-0	$12.95
Dreams of Glory: Women of the Old West Larry D. Underwood, ISBN 1-886225-15-X	$10.95
Love & Glory: Women of the Old West Larry D. Underwood, ISBN 1-886225-21-4	$10.95
Guns, Gold, & Glory Larry D. Underwood, ISBN 0939644-87-8	$9.95
The Custer Fight and Other Tales of the Old West Larry D. Underwood, ISBN 0-939644-40-1	$9.95
The Butternut Guerillas Larry D. Underwood, ISBN 0-9637515-8-1	$14.95
Evil Obsession: The Annie Cook Story Nellie Snyder Yost, ISBN 1-886225-28-1	$19.95
The Moccasin Speaks Arlene Feldmann Jauken, ISBN 1-886225-26-5	$24.95
I Am Bound For California: *The Overland Diary of Edgar Reynolds* Robert Manley, ISBN 1-886225-12-5	$10.00
Notes on Nebraska Robert Manley, ISBN 1-886225-24-9	$7.99
My Search for the Burial Sites of Sioux Nation Chiefs Veryl Walstrom, ISBN 1-886225-0905	$15.00
My First 81 Years Dorcas Cavett, ISBN 1-886225-33-8	$14.95
Amazing Tales of the Old West Jeff O'Donnell, ISBN 1-886225-17-6	$14.95

Please send:

_____ copies of _____ at $ _____
(Title of book)

_____ copies of _____ at $ _____
(Title of book)

_____ copies of _____ at $ _____
(Title of book)

_____ copies of _____ at $ _____
(Title of book)

TOTAL _____

Nebr. residents add 5% sales tax _____
Shipping/Handling
$3.50 for first book. _____
$1.00 for each additional book. _____

TOTAL ENCLOSED _____

Name _____

Address _____

City _____ State _____ Zip _____

☐ Visa ☐ MasterCard

Credit card number _____

Expiration date _____

Order by credit card, personal check or money order.

Send to:

Dageforde Publishing, Inc.
122 South 29th Street
Lincoln, NE 68510
Or, order **TOLL FREE:**
1-800-216-8794
Quantity Discounts Available